The Gita Happiness Retreat

The Gita Happiness Retreat

Retreat

Discover 40 Life Learning Lessons from The Bhagavad Gita

by

Sheetal Khurana

Vij Books India Pvt Ltd

New Delhi

Published by

Vij Books India Pvt Ltd
(Publishers, Distributors & Importers)
2/19, Ansari Road
Delhi – 110 002
Phones: 91-11-43596460, 91-11-47340674
Mobile: 98110-94883
e-mail: contact@vijpublishing.com
web: www.vijbooks.com

First Published : 2020

ISBN: 978-93-89620-15-3 (Paperback)
ISBN: 978-93-89620-16-0 (ebook)

The views expressed in this book are those of the author in her personal capacity. These do not have any institutional endorsement.

I would like to dedicate this book, with deep respect and great love, to Lord Krishna. I am grateful to Him for giving me this great opportunity to write about 'The Bhagavad Gita' and be able to serve Him and His people by spreading awareness of His teachings for the modern society.

Contents

The Gayatri Mantra

Om Bhoor Bhuvah Svah
Tat Savitur Varenyam
Bhargo Devasya Dheemahi
Dhiyo Yonah Prachodayaat

Oh Creator of the Universe
We meditate upon Thy Supreme splendor
May Thy radiant power illuminate our intellects,
Destroy our sins, and guide us in the right direction!

Introduction

On a beautiful Friday afternoon, I landed in Goa and soon checked into a beautiful and luxurious resort next to the beach. I was here to conduct a two-day spiritual retreat program based on the teaching of The Bhagavad Gita.

After settling down from a long journey I thought of checking the resort and the venue that was set up for the spiritual program. The resort was vibrating with positive energy and guests were having a gala time some were with families, some newly married couples, some were in a group and some were all by themselves. I also met the yoga trainer, coordinator and co-host of this program. After having dinner at the resort's fine dining restaurant, I sat in the lobby for some time, as that was the only place where I could get free access to Wi-Fi. The lobby was connected to two fine dining restaurants and a lounge.

Soon my eyes landed on a beautiful woman sitting in the lounge. She was looking beautiful, stunning and gorgeous wearing a short black dress. She seemed to be alone and was drinking like there is no tomorrow. I noticed she was also smoking and could make out that she was taking drugs too. Soon a guy came up to her talked to her for some time, wrote some number on a tissue paper and disappeared. After some time, the woman got up, falling wobbling walked out of the lounge towards the rooms. I don't know why, but I thought of following her thinking she might need some help. She then stopped in front of room no. 102 and rang the bell. It was clear that she didn't go to her room but to the room of the guy who wrote his room number on the tissue paper. The girl entered the room and anyone can guess what could have happened inside that room that night. I went back to my room waiting for the spiritual session to begin tomorrow.

I woke up at 6.30 am and went on the beach for a morning walk. As I went a little ahead on the beach I saw the same woman wearing the same black dress she wore last night sitting and crying profusely on the beach. Her face was swollen and her kajal was spread all over her face. I stopped by her and asked what happened. She was reluctant to even face me and cried nonstop. I sat next to her trying to pacify her. I introduced myself thinking she might stop crying and would try to talk to me. She did stop crying, looked at me but didn't utter a word. I asked her name and she said, "Shikha". I told her, "Listen I am here to conduct a two day spiritual program why don't you join in. I am a complete stranger to you, but just join in for your own good if you don't like it you are free to leave anytime. There is a yoga session happening for all the participants of our program. If you wish to join you can else just change and come here after an hour to join me for a fun session on the beach."

She did turn up on the beach exactly at 8am. "Good morning everyone, I welcome you all to this very special spiritual retreat in Ggggggoooooaaaaaaa." "I am going to pass this ball to each one of you, just tell us your name where you have come from and what made you join this spiritual program." There were 25 participants, everyone introduced himself or herself, so did Shikha.

The fun session begins. "Everyone come close and listen up carefully. Each of you need to pick up one dirty coal basket, run collect water and pour it into this bucket kept here on the sands in front of the shack. Whoever fills the bucket close to the red line in 5 minutes will be the winner of this game. Note even though this is not a group game this is your game, do what it takes to win and your time starts now." Everyone started running and were enjoying, playing, falling, laughing during this fun game. The moment they used to fill the coal basket and run towards the bucket, the water would leak from the basket. Some used different strategies formed a team, placed their hands below to stop the water from leaking and could manage filling the bucket with some water. The game came to an end. I informed them, "The winners of this game will be announced in the beginning of the spiritual program. Please carry your coal baskets and hand it over to me at the training room. You can go back to your rooms, get ready, have breakfast at the resort restaurant and we shall all meet at seminar hall 02 on the 1st floor at 10 am sharp."

It was 10 am and everyone was assembled in the seminar hall. I was again happy to see Shikha join in. "I again welcome you all to this spiritual retreat program which is based on the teaching of The Bhagavad Gita. Before we begin let me set some ground rules of this program.

1. I request everyone to keep your mobile phones on silent mode. Will give you all 15 sec to do so.

2. You are not allowed to move in and out of the training room. You can do so when we take a short break after 2 hours or at the time of games or activities.

3. You can make a note of any question coming to your mind and ask me by raising your hand or at the end of each session.

4. I would encourage everyone to write notes during the training session.

5. Keep smiling always and let's start with full josh and positive energy.

I asked everyone, "How many of you have read The Bhagavad Gita?" Very few hands were up. "How many of you know a bit about The Bhagavad Gita?" Many more hands showed up. "Can everyone tell me something about The Bhagavad Gita?" One participant said, "It is an ancient holy book of Hindu dharma. The Gita has eighteen (18) chapters and a total of only 700 verses."

I continued saying, "Okay let me tell you about The Bhagavad Gita in short. The Bhagavad Gita is a spiritual and sacred talk between the Supreme Lord Krishna and His devotee friend Arjuna, which occurs not in a temple, nor in a lonely forest, or on a mountaintop, but on a battlefield on the eve of a war.

There are 4 main Characters in the Bhagavad Gita:

1. **Lord Krishna**: He is the Principle Character of the Bhagavad Gita. Krishna is one of the human forms or avatars of Lord Vishnu.

2. **Arjuna**: He is one of the Pandava brothers and an expert archer. He represents the first method and is the direct receiver of the teachings of the Gita. First method means to have stood face-to-face with God and conversed with Him. Arjuna was a blessed soul who was given the rare honor and privilege by Lord Krishna.

3. **Sanjaya**: He was the Blind King Dhritarashtra's charioteer and secretary. He represents the second method. He was a man of immense spiritual strength who had mastered his body and mind to such an extent that they became perfect vehicles to receive the divine knowledge. He was student of sage Vyasa, and by his mercy, Sanjaya received spiritual vision because of which he was able to envision the Battlefield of Kurukshetra even while he was in the room of Dhritarashtra.

4. **Dhritarashtra**: The Blind King and the father of the wicked Kaurava brothers. He receives knowledge through the word of Sanjay. Dhritarashtra received the knowledge through the third and the most common method from another person from Sanjaya.

"The Bhagavad Gita is part of the epic Mahabharata. Would anyone like to share the story of Mahabharata in short?" One participant got up and narrated the story,

"The Mahabharata:

In ancient times there was a King who had two sons, Dhritarashtra and Pandu. The former was born blind; therefore, Pandu inherited the kingdom. Pandu had five sons. They were called the Pandavas. Dhritarashtra had one hundred sons and 1 daughter. They were called the Kauravas. Duryodhana was the eldest of the Kauravas.

After the death of King Pandu, his eldest son, Yudhisthira, became the lawful King. Duryodhana was very jealous. He also wanted the kingdom. The kingdom was divided into two halves between the Pandavas and the Kauravas. Duryodhana was not satisfied with his share. He wanted the entire kingdom for himself. He tried several evil plots to kill the Pandavas and take away their kingdom. Somehow, he took over the entire kingdom of the Pandavas and refused to give it back without a war. All peace talks by Lord Krishna who was maternal cousin of the Pandavas and others failed, so the big war of Mahabharata could not be avoided.

The Pandavas didn't want to fight, but they had only two choices: fight for their right because it was their duty or run away from war and accept defeat for the sake of peace and nonviolence. Arjuna, one of the five Pandava brothers, faced this choice on the battlefield.

He had to choose between fighting the war and killing his most esteemed guru, grandfather, who was on the other side, his very dear friends, close relatives, and many innocent warriors; or running away from the battlefield to be peaceful and nonviolent. The entire eighteen chapters of the Gita are the talk between confused Arjuna and his best friend, mentor and cousin, Lord Krishna --- an incarnation of God --- on the battlefield of Kurukshetra near New Delhi, India, about 5,100 years ago. This conversation was reported to the blind King, Dhritarashtra, by his charioteer, Sanjay. It is recorded in the great epic, Mahabharata."

"Now let's hear some opinions from all of you regarding The Bhagavad Gita". One participant said, "I find it difficult to read." The other said, "It's quite boring. One cannot understand it much." Another said, "I cannot connect it in today's times."

"Okay. By now I am sure you all are keen to know about me. Let me tell you my story and what inspired me to write the Bhagavad Gita.

One day God was very upset He was moving from one corner to the other, so His assistant asked Him, "God what happened, why are you so disturbed?" God said, "My dearest loving angel is going to earth and I'm going to miss her." Well, that's what my friends say about me that I'm a very caring, loving and a happy-go-lucky angel.

Dad kept my name Sheetal Khurana. Sheetal means cool and Khurana means that I come from a Punjabi family. I am born and bought up in Pune. I did my schooling from ICSE board then moved to SSC board. Further I went on to complete engineering from Pune. You see I was amongst those students who were not eligible for placements, little did I know that right after one year of college I will start my own recruitment consultancy firm with the help of a very senior experienced retired trainer as my partner. Unfortunately, he expired after 3 years. But I still remember his teachings: keep reading books, keep learning and I kept reading and continued my journey as an HR consultant for 14 years.

My family includes my father, my brother, my sister-in-law and my nephew. About my mother, I want to share an incident that changed my life forever. When I was 19 years old, my mom met with an accident, she suffered spinal cord injury and became paraplegic for life. My entire family was devastated; especially my mom when she came to know that she will be on wheelchair for the rest of her life.

One day a saint came to my house to see my mom. I asked him, "Why did this thing happen to us? What wrong did we do? Why did God do this? Is God really there?" But he could not answer. I was angry and didn't understand what to do. Then suddenly, one day a book landed in my hands. It was The Bhagavad Gita. By looking at the book it was saying to me, the answers to your questions are right here. Now reading the Bhagavad Gita was a very big challenge for me. I thought why not start reading just 1 page or 1-2 Shlokas translated in English everyday like a prayer. It's been 15 years till date of consistent reading and my life has changed completely. I have become more calm, wise, happy, fearless and intelligent. You all must be wondering what happened to my mother, she passed away after suffering for 4 years. Didn't I get angry with God? Well, the answer is no, I just thanked God for relieving her from the sufferings and may God bless her soul.

One day, I asked myself, what is it that I really wanted to do before I die? Yes, I wanted to write the Bhagavad Gita. I had no idea how I will write, but somehow I started writing and slowly it transformed into a bold, simple and beautiful book. Every page just tells me that its teachings can change lives and help people in today's times. This book "The Gita Happiness Retreat" is truly a gift to mankind. Here comes the first life lesson.

Lesson No: 1 Do whatever your heart tells you to do, just do it consistently and see miracles unfold.

As we all now know a bit about The Bhagavad Gita. Let's move on to Chapter 1 of The Bhagavad Gita. Immediately one participant raised his hand, got up and asked, "Madam who is the winner of the coal basket and bucket game which we all played in the morning." I smiled and said, "Each and everyone of you is the winner." All the participants were perplexed and they all looked at each other. One participant got up and said, "How is it possible, madam. Many of them couldn't fill the bucket with water, few of us together joined hands tried to fill the bucket to some extent." I smiled again and said, "Let me share a story with all of you.

Become Pure By Reading The Bhagavad Gita

On a Sunday early evening a family of four grandfather, grandson, father and mother went on a beach to have a barbeque dinner. They carried their own barbeque set along with coal required to cook. The grandfather had gifted his grandson The Bhagavad Gita on his birthday that happened few months ago. The grandson came up to him and said, "Grandpa I try to read The Bhagavad Gita just like you but I don't understand it much. And whatever little I understand, I forget it very soon. What is the use of reading this book?"

Grandfather quietly went near the barbeque set and returned with a coal basket and said, "Take this coal basket go down to the beach and bring me back a basket of water."

The young boy did as he was told, but all the water leaked out before he got back. The grandfather asked him to try again and again. But every single time, the water leaked out of the basket before he got back. Finally he got exhausted and said, "See grandpa, it's useless!"

"So you think it's useless?" The grandfather said, "Look at the basket." The boy looked at the basket and for the first time realized that the basket had been transformed from a dirty coal basket to a new clean one, inside and out.

"Son, that's what happens when you read a book like the Bhagavad Gita. You might not understand or remember everything, but when you read it again and again, you will realize the benefit one day. It will help you become pure from the inside and outside, just like this coal basket."

All the participants looked at their clean coal basket, smiled and gave a big applaud. I said, "Everyone is a winner and what did you all win?" Another life lesson.

**Lesson No: 2 Read this beautiful sacred book The Bhagavad Gita consistently. Try to understand its teachings and do your own research. The sacred texts have a purpose that will help you find your true purpose in life and also help you find solutions to your problems.

CHAPTER 1

Arjuna Is Confused

"Let's continue the session.

You all have a note pad which is given to you along with a pen. I want you to write down the names of all the people who matter to you, including your own name? Time is 1 minute.

Okay times up. Please count and tell me numbers randomly on your list. Anyone. Some said, "15, 20, 25, 40". Now I want you to think and circle those names whom you are very close to, rest cross the remaining. Time is 15 sec. Please count and tell me numbers randomly on your list. Anyone. Some said, "3, 5, 7, 10". Aren't they you, your family and friends? Everyone nodded. Anyone crossed their own name?" Thankfully there was no one.

"In the two day spiritual session we are going to understand the importance of relationships and how to manage them with the help of The Bhagavad Gita.

There are 46 Shlokas in Chapter 1 of The Bhagavad Gita. I request each participant to read one shloka each that is translated in English. Here is The Bhagavad Gita." Everyone started reading one after the other.

Observing the Armies on the Battlefield of Kurukshetra:

Dhritarashtra said: O Sanjaya, after my sons and the sons of Pandu assembled in the place of pilgrimage at Kurukshetra, desiring to fight, what did they do?

Sanjaya said: O King, after looking over the army arranged in military formation by the sons of Pandu, King Duryodhana went to his teacher Dronacharya and spoke the following words.

O my teacher, observe the great army of the sons of Pandu, so expertly arranged by your intelligent disciple the son of Drupada.

Here in this army are many brave archers equal in fighting to Bhima and Arjuna: great fighters like Yuyudhana, Virata and Drupada.

There are also great heroic, powerful fighters like Dhrishtaketu, Chekitana, Kashiraja, Purujit, Kuntibhoja and Saibya.

There are the mighty Yudhamanyu, the very powerful Uttamauja, the son of Subhadra and the sons of Draupadi. All these warriors are great chariot fighters.

But for your information, O best of the brahmanas let me tell you about the captains who are especially qualified to lead my military force.

There are personalities like you, Bhishma, Karna, Kripa, Ashvatthama, Vikarna and the son of Somadatta called Bhurishravas, who are always victorious in battle.

There are many other heroes who are prepared to lay down their lives for my sake. All of them are well equipped with different kinds of weapons, and all are experienced in military science.

Our strength is immeasurable, and we are perfectly protected by Grandfather Bhishma, whereas the strength of the Pandavas, carefully protected by Bhima, is limited.

All of you must now give full support to Grandfather Bhishma, as you stand at your respective strategic points into the phalanx of the army.

Then Bhishma, the great courageous grandfather of the Kuru dynasty, the grandfather of the fighters, blew his conchshell very loudly, making a sound like the roar of a lion, giving Duryodhana joy.

After that, the conchshells, drums, bugles, trumpets and horns were all suddenly sounded and the combined sound was thunderous.

On the other side, both Lord Krishna and Arjuna, stationed on a great chariot drawn by white horses, sounded their transcendental (superior) conchshells.

Lord Krishna blew His conchshell, called Panchajanya; Arjuna blew his, the Devadatta; and Bhima, the voracious eater and performer of difficult tough tasks, blew his terrific conchshell called Paundra.

King Yudhishthira, the son of Kunti, blew his conchshell, the Anantavijaya, and Nakula and Sahadeva blew the Sughosh and Manipushpak. That great archer the King of Kasi, the great fighter Shikhandi, Dhrishtadyumna, Virata and the unconquerable Satyaki, Drupada, the sons of Draupadi, and others, O King, such as the mighty-armed son of Subhadra, all blew their respective conchshells.

The blowing of these different conchshells became uproarious. Vibrating both in the sky and on the earth, it shattered the hearts of the sons of Dhritarashtra.

At that time Arjuna, the son of Pandu, seated in the chariot bearing the flag marked with Hanuman, took up his bow and prepared to shoot his arrows. O King, after looking at the sons of Dhritarashtra drawn in military array, Arjuna then spoke to Lord Krishna these words.

Arjuna said: O flawless one, please draw my chariot between the two armies so that I may see those present here, who desire to fight, and with whom I must take on in this great battle.

Let me see those who have come here to fight, wishing to please the evil-minded son of Dhritarashtra.

Sanjaya said: O descendant of Bharata, having thus been addressed by Arjuna, Lord Krishna drew up the fine chariot in the midst of the armies of both parties.

In the presence of Bhishma, Drona and all the other chieftains of the world, Lord Krishna said, just observe, Partha, all the Kurus assembled here.

There Arjuna could see, within the midst of the armies of both parties, his fathers, grandfathers, teachers, maternal uncles, brothers, sons, grandsons, friends, and also his father-in-law and well-wishers.

When the son of Kunti, Arjuna, saw all these different grades of friends and relatives, he became very emotional with compassion and spoke thus.

Arjuna said: My dear Krishna, seeing my friends and relatives present before me in such a fighting spirit, I feel the limbs of my body quivering and my mouth drying up.

My whole body is trembling, my hair is standing on end, my bow Gandiva is slipping from my hand, and my skin is burning.

I am now unable to stand here any longer. I am forgetting myself, and my mind is loosing its balance. I see only causes of misfortune, O Krishna, killer of the Keshi demon.

I do not see how any good can come from killing my own kinsmen in this battle, nor can I, my dear Krishna, desire any subsequent victory, kingdom, or happiness.

O Govinda, of what avail to us are a kingdom, happiness or even life itself when all those for whom we may desire them are now assembled on this battlefield? O Madhusudana, when teachers, fathers, sons, grandfathers, maternal uncles, fathers-in-law, grandsons, brothers-in-law and other relatives are ready to give up their lives and properties and are standing before me, why should I wish to kill them, even though they might otherwise kill me? O maintainer of all living entities, I am not prepared to fight with them even in exchange for the three worlds, let alone this earth. What pleasure will we derive from killing the sons of Dhritarashtra?

Sin will overcome us if we slay such aggressors. Therefore, it is not proper for us to kill the sons of Dhritarashtra and our friends. What should we gain, O Krishna, husband of the goddess of fortune, and how could we be happy by killing our own kinsmen?

O Janardana, although these men, their hearts overtaken by greed, see no fault in killing one's family or quarreling with friends, why should we, who can see the crime in destroying a family, engage in these acts of sin?

With the destruction of dynasty, the never-ending family tradition is vanquished, and thus the rest of the family becomes involved in irreligion.

When irreligion is prominent in the family, O Krishna, the women of the family become polluted, and from the degradation of womanhood, O descendant of Vrishni, comes unwanted children.

An increase of unwanted population certainly causes hellish life both for the family and for those who destroy the family tradition. The ancestors of such corrupt families fall down, because the performances for offering them food and water are entirely stopped.

By the evil deeds of those who destroy the family tradition and thus give rise to unwanted children, all kinds of community projects and family welfare activities are devastated.

O Krishna, maintainer of the people, I have heard by disciplic succession that those who destroy family traditions dwell always in hell.

Alas, how strange it is that we are preparing to commit greatly sinful acts. Driven by the desire to enjoy royal happiness, we are determined on killing our own kinsmen.

Better for me if the sons of Dhritarashtra, weapons in hand, were to kill me unarmed and unresisting on the battlefield.

Sanjaya said: Arjuna, having thus spoken on the battlefield, cast aside his bow and arrows and sat down on the chariot, his mind overwhelmed with grief.

Now let me Summarize Chapter 1:

As both the armies stand well positioned for battle, Arjuna asked his charioteer friend Lord Krishna, to drive his chariot between the two armies so that he could see the Kaurvas army. Arjuna felt great compassion after seeing his relatives, teachers and friends on the opposite side ready to fight and sacrifice their lives. He must kill them to win the war. Overcome by grief and pity of having to kill his own blood relatives, Arjuna's body started to tremble, his mind loosing its balance, he became confused. Arjuna got completely immersed in grief caused by attachment and delusion. He started speaking about the evils of war causing destruction of the dynasty; he simply refused and gave up his determination to fight.

I asked, "Can anyone tell me what's wrong with Arjuna?" One participant replied, "Confused fight or not to fight". The other said, "He thinks it's better not to fight this war, this way he won't need to kill his own blood relatives." Another participant said, "He felt compassion when he saw his blood relatives ready to lay down their lives and properties to win this war." One more participant said, "He was overcome with feelings of grief and pity". One participant asked, "How is this relevant today?"

I said, "Let me share a story with all of you.

Special Horse That Always Wins The Race

One day at a restaurant, I happened to overhear a conversation between two friends. One friend said, "I am not able to stick to one relationship, I have changed three girlfriends in 6 months." The other friend then said, "Let me share a story with you about a special horse that always wins the race.

Once there was a rich man who used to place bets on different horses in every race. Everyone was surprised to see him winning every time. So, one gentleman went up to him and asked him, "Sir what's your secret to winning? How is it that you know exactly which is the special horse that will win the race?" The rich man smiled and said, "It's a secret! When the horses are not racing, I keep a watch on them all the time, I talk to them and I also feed them." The gentleman asked, "But what's the connection, I didn't understand." The rich man replied, "I decide which special horse will win the upcoming race. I start by feeding that special horse with good food. To the rest of the horses I make them starve or feed them with less food. Also, I talk positive things with that special horse by using encouraging, motivating words and with remaining I talk negative and depressing words. The result is what I get winning on the special horse that I feed with good food and positive talks."

The other friend looked at his friend and asked, "So what did you learn from this?" First friend said, "It means we too can win in our lives, when we feed ourselves as well as our mind with good, positive thoughts and positive words. For that first I need to become good friends with the girl I really like and then invest decent time to get to know her and then decide to be in a relationship with that girl. Think positive about our relationship. Only by feeding my mind with positive thoughts, will help me achieve success in a relationship."

The other friend said, "Very well said and learnt. The point of the story is that if we want a stable relationship or a stable life and a balanced mind, we need to feed our mind with positive thoughts. So that we can experience happiness, joy and peace, plus we will be able to achieve whatever we want in our life. If we feed our mind with negative thoughts, we will end up experiencing negativity such as stress, anxiety, fear, anger and sadness. Which will lead us nowhere but to confusion. Imagine achieving success by becoming that special horse that always wins the race.

One participant raised his hand and said, "It's easy to say think positive but practically things don't go as planned or as imagined. Our relatives, family, friends, bosses, colleagues, clients, customers or some outsider are just waiting to bark negative thoughts at us and we like fools keep thinking about it over and over again in turn getting ourselves disturbed, sad and upset. So what's the solution to this?"

I asked everyone, "Let me all ask you a question? If some unknown guest comes to your house knocks at your door, what do you do? Do you just open the door and let that person in or do you see through the keyhole? Of course you see through the keyhole first. Similarly, first we need to find out that negative thought is knocking at your door, how do we do this? By seeing through our inner keyhole. That's nothing but our "Awareness". Second thing is to not let it enter your home that's your mind, how do we do this? By refusing to think about it and telling it to go away, automatically it will go away when you start focusing on the special horse that always wins the race.

I myself have experienced being in trap, feeling sometimes positive and most of the time negative, having mood swings, didn't really understand what to do. When I asked my friends to help me. One said, "Make it a point that you do not listen to negative talks at all, this will help you stay positive and happy always". The other friend said, "Think positive in every negative situation you experience". My best friends taught me how to keep thinking about the special horse that always wins the race.

Finally, this story of the special horse that always wins the race also closely relates to the Bhagavad Gita, where Arjuna is overcome by negative thoughts of grief and pity of having to kill his own blood relatives on the battlefield of Kurukshetra and Lord Krishna helps him to think positive and guides him on how to become that special horse that always wins the race. This teaches us a very important life lesson.

Lesson No: 3 Think Positive. Feed your mind with positive thoughts always and this will help you focus on achieving success in life.

Silently a hand went up, it was Shikha. "Yes Shikha, any question?" She said, "How can we think positive if the person whom we love cheats on us?" Another participant said, "Madam Arjuna's feeling of compassion towards his relatives and not being in favor of fighting this war was positive. How is it negative?"

I said, "Is committing suicide, positive thing or negative thing?" Everyone said, "Negative thing". "Let me share another story with all of you.

A Man In Trouble

One day on a mountaintop, a man was standing right at the edge. He looked sad and depressed. Oh no! He was there to commit suicide. At that very moment Lord Krishna and Arjuna were passing by and they observed and felt that the man was up to something. So they disguised themselves as normal men and went to help him.

Arjuna asked, "What are you trying to do?"

The man said, "I am fed up of my life and want to commit suicide."

Arjuna asked, "But why? Kindly share your problems with us may be we can help."

So the man said, "My wife has cheated on me. I cannot accept this fact and cannot see her with someone else. I love her very much so want to release her as well as myself from this stress."

Arjuna said, "Committing suicide is not the right thing to do or even to think about. For every problem there is a solution. We must never loose hope and never give up. Have you ever thought what will happen to your family after you commit suicide."

"No human being on this earth is free from problems. We must learn to face our problems and not run away from it. Just think what if you commit suicide now and again in next life you are faced with the same or even worse problems, then what will you do? Commit suicide again. Just think about it."

Lord Krishna who was silently listening to this conversation said, "Let me help you by sharing the solutions to your problems."

Lord Krishna looked at the man and said, "My friend are you 100% sure that your wife has cheated on you. Have you spoken with her on this matter. Has she admitted that she has cheated on you?"

"If your answer is no, then do not worry. Go home and talk with your wife openly on this matter."

"But, if your answer is yes and your wife is guilty of her deed and she wants you to forgive her. My friend, please go ahead forgive her and forget about what happened and move on in your life. I know it will be difficult in the beginning but try to look at the positive side of the person, think of all the good she has done for you and ignore the negatives."

"Look at it this way. Couples who get divorced on various reasons, don't they get remarried and accept their new spouse irrespective of their past relationships?

The man asked what if I forgive her now but later she again cheats on me. Lord Krishna smiled and said, "My friend, our body be it a man or a woman is made up of senses which is not in our control. It is controlled by nature. If she cheats on you, talk to her with an open mind. Give her your help, support, love, patience, time and find solution to this problem. Over a period of time, she will realize your love and everything will be fine in your life. If you continue to face issues and you are unable to handle this emotional stress, then my friend your heart will guide you in the right direction. There are two choices in front of you, either you accept her and forgive whatever happened or leave her and move on in your life. Just listen to what your heart says, take the right step and your problems will get sorted out."

The man was surprised to hear such a point of view and didn't know how to thank Lord Krishna for this. The man said, "I am very grateful to You for showing me the right direction. My stress has gone. Thank you for guiding me."

That man then went back to his home with a big smile.

Arjuna asked Lord Krishna, "Had we not seen him at the right time, he would have surely committed suicide. But who will help people like him when we are not there?"

Lord Krishna said, "People don't realize that their family and friends are actual messengers sent by Me to help them. But in today's time, people underestimate them and refuse to seek guidance and help because of their ego or of feeling ashamed or embarrassed about what they will think."

Lord Krishna then said to Arjuna, "Do you remember what happened to you on the battlefield of Kurukshetra? You too were feeling sad, depressed and refused to fight after seeing your blood relatives on the battlefield. Similarly we all feel compassion towards our loved ones and when problems arise we don't understand what to do, we feel devastated we loose hope and give up. We even refuse to get up and fight for ourselves. So my dearest friend all you need to do is think positive and be determined to find solutions to your problems."

Everyone in the session looked dumbfounded after hearing this story. I looked at Shikha and first time saw her smile. This made me really happy.

Here comes another life lesson.

**Lesson No: 4 Remember everyone has problems. Discuss your problems with your loved ones. Look for solutions. Never let go the person whom you love.

CHAPTER 2

Arjuna Surrenders To Lord Krishna

"Let's move on to the next chapter. Chapter 2 has 72 shlokas. I request each participant to read two shlokas each that is translated in English." Everyone started reading one after the other.

Contents of the Gita Summarized

Sanjaya said: Seeing Arjuna full of compassion, his mind depressed, his eyes full of tears, Madhusudana, Krishna, spoke the following words.

The Supreme Personality of Godhead said: My dear Arjuna, how have these impurities come upon you? They are not at all appropriate to a man who knows the value of life. They lead not to higher planets but to disgrace.

O son of Pritha, do not surrender to this degrading inability to take action. It does not become you. Give up such petty weakness of heart and arise, O chastiser of the enemy.

Arjuna said: O killer of enemies, O killer of Madhu, how can I counterattack with arrows in battle men like Bhishma and Drona, who are worthy of my worship?

It would be better to live in this world by begging than to live at the cost of the lives of great souls who are my teachers. Even though desiring worldly gain, they are superiors. If they are killed, everything we enjoy will be tainted with blood.

Nor do we know which is better conquering them or being conquered by them. If we killed the sons of Dhritarashtra, we should not care to live. Yet they are now standing before us on the battlefield.

Now I am confused about my duty and have lost all composure because of pitiful weakness. In this condition I am asking You to tell me for certain what is best for me. Now I am Your disciple, and a soul surrendered unto You. Please instruct me.

I can find no means to drive away this grief, which is drying up my senses. I will not be able to get rid of it even if I win a prosperous, unbeaten kingdom on earth with supreme power like the demigods in heaven.

Sanjaya said: Having spoken thus, Arjuna, chastiser of enemies, told Krishna, "Govinda, I shall not fight," and fell silent.

O descendant of Bharata, at that time Krishna, smiling, in the midst of both the armies, spoke the following words to the grief-stricken Arjuna.

The Supreme Personality of Godhead said: While speaking learned words, you are mourning for what is not worthy of grief. Those who are wise cry neither for the living nor for the dead.

Never was there a time when I did not exist, nor you, nor all these kings; nor in the future shall any of us cease to be.

As the embodied soul continually passes, in this body, from boyhood to youth to old age, the soul similarly passes into another body at death. A sober person is not confused by such a change.

O son of Kunti, the nonpermanent appearance of happiness and sorrow, and their disappearance in due course, are like the appearance and disappearance of winter and summer seasons. They arise from sense awareness, O descendant of Bharata, and one must learn to tolerate them without being disturbed.

O best among men [Arjuna], the person who is not disturbed by happiness and sorrow and is steady in both is certainly eligible for freedom.

Those who are seers of the truth have concluded that of the material body there is no permanence, and of the eternal [the soul] there is no change. This they have concluded by studying the nature of both.

That which spreads through the entire body you should know to be indestructible. No one is able to destroy the imperishable soul.

The material body of the indestructible, immeasurable and eternal living entity is sure to come to an end; therefore, fight, O descendant of Bharata.

Neither he who thinks the living entity is the killer nor he who thinks it has killed is in knowledge, for the self [soul] kills not nor is killed.

For the soul there is neither birth nor death at any time. He has not come into being, does not come into being, and will not come into being. He is unborn, eternal, ever existing and original. He is not killed when the body is killed.

O Partha, how can a person who knows that the soul is indestructible, eternal, unborn and permanent kill anyone or cause anyone to kill?

As a person puts on new garments, giving up old ones, the soul similarly accepts new material bodies, giving up the old and useless ones.

The soul can never be cut into pieces by any weapon, nor burned by fire, nor moistened by water, nor dried by the wind.

This individual soul is unbreakable and insoluble, and can be neither burned nor dried. He is everlasting, present everywhere, unchangeable, immovable and eternally the same.

It is said that the soul is invisible, unimaginable and permanent. Knowing this, you should not grieve for the body.

If, however, you think that the soul is always born and dies forever, you still have no reason to moan, O mighty-armed.

For one who has taken his birth is sure to die, and after death one is sure to take birth again. Therefore, in the unavoidable discharge of your duty, you should not moan.

All created beings are invisible in their beginning, visible in their temporary state, and invisible again when they are destroyed. So what need is there for sorrow?

Some look on the soul as amazing, some describe him as amazing, and some hear of him as amazing, while others, even after hearing about him, cannot understand him at all.

O descendant of Bharata, he who lives in the body can never be killed. Therefore, you need not grieve for any living being.

Considering your specific duty as a Kshatriya, you should know that there is no better engagement for you than fighting on religious principles; and so there is no need for hesitation.

O Partha, happy are the Kshatriyas to whom such fighting opportunities come unsought, opening for them the doors of the heavenly planets.

If, however, you do not perform your religious duty of fighting, then you will certainly incur sins for neglecting your duties and thus lose your reputation as a fighter.

People will always speak of your disgrace, and for a respectable person, dishonor is worse than death.

The great generals who have highly esteemed your name and fame will think that you have left the battlefield out of fear only, and thus they will consider you worthless.

Your enemies will describe you in many unkind words and mock at your ability. What could be more painful for you?

O son of Kunti, either you will be killed on the battlefield and attain the heavenly planets, or you will conquer and enjoy the earthly kingdom. Therefore, get up with determination and fight.

Do fight for the sake of fighting, without considering happiness or sorrow, loss or gain, victory or defeat-and by so doing you shall never incur sin.

Thus far I have described this knowledge to you through analytical study. Now listen as I explain it in terms of working without fruitive results. O son of Pritha, when you act in such knowledge you can free yourself from the bondage of works.

In this attempt there is no loss or decline, and a little advancement on this path can protect one from the most dangerous type of fear.

Those who are on this path are determined in purpose, and their aim is one. O beloved child of the Kurus, the intelligence of those who are uncertain is many-branched.

Men of small knowledge are very much attached to the flowery words of the Vedas, which recommend various fruitive activities for elevation to heavenly planets, resultant good birth, power, and so *forth. Being desirous of sense pleasure and luxurious life, they say that there is nothing more than this.*

In the minds of those who are too attached to sense enjoyment and material richness, and who are confused by such things, the unwavering determination for devotional service to the Supreme Lord does not take place.

The Vedas deal mainly with the subject of the three modes of material nature. O Arjuna, become transcendental (superior) to these three modes. Be free from all dualities and from all anxieties for gain and safety, and be established in the self.

All purposes that are served by a small well can at once be served by a great reservoir of water. Similarly, all the purposes of the Vedas can be served to one who knows the purpose behind them.

You have a right to perform your prescribed duty, but you are not entitled to the fruits of action. Never consider yourself the cause of the results of your activities, and never be attached to not doing your duty.

Perform your duty with a balanced mind, O Arjuna, abandoning all attachment to success or failure. Such calmness is called yoga.

O Dhananjaya, keep all bad activities far distant by devotional service, and in that awareness surrender unto the Lord. Those who want to enjoy the fruits of their work are misers.

A man engaged in devotional service rids himself of both good and bad actions even in this life. Therefore, strive for yoga, O Arjuna, which is the art of all work.

By thus engaging in devotional service to the Lord, great sages or devotees free themselves from the results of work in the material world. In this way they become free from the cycle of birth and death and attain the state beyond all miseries [by going back to Godhead].

When your intelligence has passed out of the dense forest of misbelief, you shall become indifferent to all that has been heard and all that is to be heard.

When your mind is no longer disturbed by the flowery language of the Vedas, and when it remains fixed in the trance of self-realization, then you will have attained the divine consciousness.

Arjuna said: O Krishna, what are the symptoms of one whose consciousness is thus merged in transcendence (experience beyond the normal)? How does he speak, and what is his language? How does he sit, and how does he walk?

The Supreme Personality of Godhead said: O Partha, when a man gives up all varieties of desire for sense pleasure, which arise from mental creation, and when his mind, thus purified, finds satisfaction in the self alone, then he is said to be in pure transcendental consciousness.

One who is not disturbed in mind even amidst the threefold miseries or overjoyed when there is happiness, and who is free from attachment, fear and anger, is called a sage of steady mind.

In the material world, one who is unaffected by whatever good or evil he may obtain, neither praising it nor disliking it, is firmly fixed in perfect knowledge.

One who is able to withdraw his senses from sense objects, as the tortoise draws its limbs within the shell, is firmly fixed in perfect consciousness.

The embodied soul may be restricted from sense enjoyment, though the taste for sense objects remains. But, ending such engagements by experiencing a higher taste, he is fixed in consciousness.

The senses are so strong and quick, O Arjuna, that they forcibly carry away the mind even of a man of discrimination who is trying hard to control them.

One who restrains his senses, keeping them under full control, and fixes his consciousness upon Me, is known as a man of steady intelligence.

While thinking deeply about the objects of the senses, a person develops attachment for them, and from such attachment lust develops, and from lust anger arises.

From anger, complete misunderstanding arises, and from misunderstanding confusion of memory. When memory is confused, intelligence is lost, and when intelligence is lost one falls down again into the material pool.

But a person free from all attachment and hatred and able to control his senses through regulative principles of freedom can obtain the complete mercy of the Lord.

For one thus satisfied [in Krishna consciousness], the threefold miseries of material existence exist no longer; in such satisfied consciousness, one's intelligence is soon well established.

One who is not connected with the Supreme [in Krishna consciousness] can have neither transcendental (superior) intelligence nor a steady mind, without which there is no possibility of peace. And how can there be any happiness without peace?

As a strong wind sweeps away a boat on the water, even one of the roaming senses on which the mind focuses can carry away a man's intelligence.

Therefore, O mighty-armed, one whose senses are kept under control from their objects is certainly of steady intelligence.

What is night for all beings is the time of awakening for the self-controlled; and the time of awakening for all beings is night for the inward-looking sage.

A person who is not disturbed by the never-ending flow of desires-that enter like rivers into the ocean which is ever being filled but is always still-can alone achieve peace, and not the man who strives to satisfy such desires.

A person who has given up all desires for sense pleasure, who lives free from desires, who has given up all sense of proprietorship and is free from false ego-he alone can attain real peace.

That is the way of the spiritual and godly life, after attaining which a man is not confused. If one is thus situated even at the hour of death, one can enter into the kingdom of God.

Now let me Summarize Chapter 2:

Arjuna who was confused about his duty, surrenders to Lord Krishna as His disciple and requests the Lord to instruct him. Lord Krishna teaches Arjuna the difference between temporary material body and the eternal spiritual soul. Lord Krishna reminds Arjuna of his duty as a Kshatriya and encourages him to fight on religious principles. Lord also explains him the ill effects of not fighting. Lord Krishna explains the process of transmigration, the nature of soul, devotional service to the Supreme and the characteristics of a self-realized person.

He talks about how to work without fruitive results, by engaging in devotional service to the Lord and becoming free from the results of work in the material world. In this way become free from cycle of birth and death and attain the state beyond all miseries by going back to Godhead. This state is known as Krishna consciousness. When one is connected with Supreme in Krishna consciousness, he receives superior intelligence and a steady mind and from this comes the ultimate state of peace and happiness.

I asked everyone, "Can anyone tell me what do you understand from this chapter?" One participant replied, "Arjuna surrenders to Lord Krishna asking to help him or guide him". The other said, "It talks about transmigration, the difference between our body and soul." One participant asked, "How is this relevant today?" I said, "This is my favorite question, let me share something interesting with all of you.

Lifesaver

I want you all to close your eyes and imagine you are on a big ship; suddenly the ship is about to sink. Captain of the ship calls for emergency "Abort, Abort" and you jump into the water to save your life. You see a lifeboat and swim towards it. After you climbed on it, how many people do you think will be there with you on that lifeboat? 2, 5, 10, 15, 20 etc. These are exactly the number of friends you have in your life, this is according to a personality quiz that I happen to come across many many years back while surfing the Internet. Now I want you to ask yourself how many best friends do you have in your life? 0,1, 2, 3, etc. These best friends are nothing but your Lifesavers who will help you through trouble waters. So have at least 1-2 best friends in your life.

There are 4 ways to find your best friend for life.

1: Find a friend with two ears and an open heart

I came across a beautiful meme which says, 'When two ears are put side by side, it forms the shape of the heart. Interestingly, the word "ear" sits right in middle of the word "heart" (h-ear-t). The ear is the way to the heart. So, if you want to win someone's heart, learn to listen to him or her.' Sometimes in our life, we don't need any advice but just a sincere friend to talk our heart out. There is a quote that says, "Just being with your best friend, is all that you need." So have that Lifesaver who will listen to you and console you in trouble situations.

2: Find a friend who will guide you in the right direction

We all know that Lord Krishna and Arjuna were Best Friends. When the war between Kauravas and Pandavas was finalized, Duryodhana and Arjuna went to Lord Krishna for support. Lord Krishna said, "I will help you both, but to one I will give my vast army and to the other I will only give moral support because I will not fight". Arjuna immediately chose Lord Krishna because he knew with His support and guidance they will win the war and Duryodhana was too happy to have the army by his side. This was indeed the turning point in the Mahabharata, where just the presence of the Lord was needed to win the war. Arjuna surrendered himself to Lord Krishna for guidance. Similarly, we are also like Arjuna who are facing challenges in our day-to-day lives and we too need a best friend like Lord Krishna by our side to help us win inner battles, to achieve success in our lives, to live our life in happiness and peace. So have that Lifesaver, have that Best Friend who will guide you in trouble situations.

3: Find a friend whom you can trust but keep your eyes open

You see trusting someone is the most difficult thing. You feel scared what if this friend tells someone or what if he or she laughs at me or gives me a wrong advise. But the thing is unless you open your heart out, how will you know that this person can be my best friend. You finally will get two results: A best friend for life or a lesson for life. I have 2 best friends in my life for the past 20 years and 1 best friend from school. Many a times they would advise me that there is a ditch ahead of you, don't go. I used to not listen and then I would fall into the ditch. But they were always there giving their hands to pull me out of the ditch, of course after having a hefty laugh. That's what friendship is. It takes a lot of time, patience and energy to build trust. But also be careful of those friends who can take you in wrong direction. Never let anyone take advantage of you for money, love, sex, drugs or revenge. So have that Lifesaver whom you can trust, who can take you out of trouble waters but at the same time keep your eyes open on the Lifesaver, making sure he or she doesn't drown you.

4: Find a real friend who will hold your hands and give you a hug

Today we are in a technology driven environment where we have more number of friends on Facebook and Instagram than the ones close to us. We spend more time on smartphones than with people wanting to be with us. Go knock at the door of your friends, give them a hug and spend time with them. Take time out for real people because real friends hold hands not virtual ones. When you are surrounded by negative energy, your best friend will hold your hand give you a tight hug and transfer positive energy to make you feel good.

There was a girl who had many friends on Facebook but she didn't have a single best friend. As time passed by, she started feeling lonely, sad, depressed and later ended up committing suicide. I happened to ask many middle age men and women, "Do you have a best friend in your life?" The answer I received was common, "Are you kidding, at this juncture of our lives who has time for friends we are too busy with work and family." When I asked the same question to old men and women, the answer I got was, "Wish I had a best friend in my life." So have that Lifesaver who will hold your hands, give you a hug and will never leave you alone.

Arjuna was fortunate enough to have Lord Krishna by his side, on the battlefield of Kurukshetra. So when Lord Krishna saw that Arjuna is refusing to fight the war because of his feelings of compassion towards his blood relatives. He became his Lifesaver and a Best Friend who guided and motivated him to do his duty by showing him the right direction, after he surrendered to Lord Krishna asking for help.

God cannot be there everywhere, so he created a Best Friend. So let's make a new beginning by having a Best Friend in our life. With whom we not only want to party with but who is also a good listener who urges us to share our problems, who can guide us to take the right decisions in life and whom we can trust by keeping our eyes open. In this digital age of Facebook and Instagram, lets take a step forward and move from a tech life to a more human life and have a Best Friend for Life.

Everyone in the session stood up and started applauding on the simple yet wonderful life lesson.

**Lesson No: 5 Have at least 1 Best Friend in your life who will guide you in the right direction, who will help you win inner battles and help you come out of trouble situations.

Everyone sat down and then a hand went up, one participant asked, "Madam the title of chapter 2 is Contents of The Gita Summarized, how would you summarize The Bhagavad Gita?"

I said, "Would you all like to hear another interesting story that will answer this participant's question? Everyone nodded.

Famous Doctor

Once there was a doctor who was very famous. He treated patients having mental illness with a 100% success rate. The patients who went to him once for treatment never visited him again, but surely they became his ambassadors and spread his name like wild fire. The doctor became so famous that even Lord Krishna wanted to personally meet him and know his secret.

So Lord Krishna disguised Himself as a patient and went to this famous doctor and said, "Doctor I feel very lonely, depressed all the time. I also feel stressed most of the time. Because of worry and anxiety My blood pressure always remains high and sugar levels shoot up. My heart is also weak. Please help Me doctor." Doctor said, "The same problem is faced by most of the patients who come to me."

Doctor then showed Lord Krishna the picture of the sacred 'Bhagavad Gita'.

Lord Krishna smiled from within and said, "Doctor what are you trying to say, I don't understand. Please give me medicine and not this picture. How can this picture cure my problems?"

Doctor told, "Look at this picture carefully. What do you see?"

Lord Krishna said, "I see Arjuna sitting with folded hands along with Lord Krishna who is guiding him on a chariot. The chariot has four horses and Lord Krishna as charioteer holds their reins. I also see that the chariot is right in middle of the two armies with Pandavas on one side and Kauravas on the other side."

Doctor said, "Great observation."

He further continued, "Now let me explain how it is related to you and your problems and what is the medication."

Doctor said, "The two armies represents the two types of people we find in this world. Pandavas represents good and divine type of people and Kauravas represents bad and demonic type of people. We too come across both types of people in today's life. Some give us happiness like our family and friends; some gives us stress in our life. Man is continuously fighting not only between these two types of people but also within himself between what's right and wrong, good path and bad path, positive thoughts and negative thoughts."

"Arjuna represents the soul who is fighting this battle from within him. Like Arjuna we must face this life and its challenges on our own. He is praying to Lord Krishna and surrendering himself completely to the Lord for guidance and help."

"Here Lord Krishna shows us that God is always there to support and guide us. Lord Krishna is the Supreme Personality of Godhead who is situated as Paramatma in the heart of every living being. Krishna is your inner voice, inspiration and divine guidance that is continuously guiding the lost, lonely and depressed souls in the right direction. Only when you become aware of His presence within you, will you become free from all problems."

"Lord Krishna is holding the reins of the four horses. Here horses represent our senses that tend to move in different directions and are difficult to control. Only when you completely surrender yourself to Lord Krishna, He will help you take control of your mind which is the rein with which all the senses that is the horses come under control and they start moving into the right direction according to the will of the Lord."

"The chariot in between is nothing but our life. Till the time we are on this chariot, means till the time we are alive, we have to fight our own war."

Doctor further asked another question, "Do you know why was The Bhagavad Gita told in middle of both the armies? Lord Krishna said, "No, why." Doctor said, "It's because Life is all about balance."

Lord Krishna as patient was surprised to see the doctor's in-depth knowledge and philosophy. He then smiled and asked the famous doctor, "Doctor medicine please."

Doctor said, "Firstly 'Stop Worrying'. Surrender all your worries to Lord Krishna, just like how you unload a heavy baggage from your head and put it to the ground. Stop thinking negative. Have faith in Lord Krishna that He is there with you always and is just a call away and He will come to your rescue. Just imagine a Supreme Power is waiting for your instructions. Read the sacred book 'The Bhagavad Gita' daily this will bring peace in your life. Your fears will disappear. And talk your heart out about your problems to your best friend. If you don't have a best friend then find one that's your lifetime medicine."

Doctor said, "Please come back to me if your problem is not solved. But I haven't seen my patients come again."

Lord Krishna smiled and said, "Even though you have become a doctor by studying so hard. You are practicing it very truly, perfectly and performing your duty to the best of your abilities without worrying about success or failure. I bless you."

Lord Krishna then smiled and left his clinic with great satisfaction.

This knowledge and philosophy holds true in today's times, wherein man is struggling with the war going on within himself, he is overcome by negative thoughts and fear all the time. Because of negative thoughts he is unable to fulfill his desires and dreams. This is precisely leading him to sadness and depression. Only when you truly surrender yourself to Lord Krishna, you will be able to control your strong senses with the help of your mind by focusing on the right and positive thoughts. Your inner guiding light Lord Krishna will guide you in the right direction."

After hearing this story, everyone in the session carefully looked at the picture I showed on the ppt. I then asked everyone, "What is the life lesson from this story?"

**Lesson No: 6 Do not let negative thoughts take control of you. You have to overcome challenges and fight your own war. Use your mind to control your senses by focusing on the right and positive thoughts.

CHAPTER 3

Arjuna Do Your Work

"Are you all liking this spiritual session on The Bhagavad Gita?" Yes is what I hear. "Great. How do you find this training room, good okay bad?" Good is what I hear. "How are the chairs, comfortable okay not bad?" Comfortable is what I hear. "Okay now what if one leg of the chair breaks, what will happen?" One participant said, "The person sitting on that chair will fall down." I asked, "Anyone else wants to say something more, please share." Another participant said, "Everyone will laugh when that person falls down." Yet another participant said, "That person will feel embarrassed." I asked everyone, "What do you think that leg of the chair represents in our life?" Someone said, "Health", other participant said, "Wealth". Another participant said, "Personal life" and one said, "Work life". There was a naughty participant who said, "Sex life" and everyone laughed. "The answer is what one participant said very correctly, it's our Work life."

"Chapter 3 of The Bhagavad Gita talks about your work life. This chapter has 43 shlokas. I request each participant to read one shloka each that is translated in English." Everyone started reading one after the other.

Karma Yoga

Arjuna said: O Janardana, O Keshava, why do You want to engage me in this awful warfare, if You think that intelligence is better than fruitive work?

My intelligence is confused by Your unclear opposing instructions. Therefore, please tell me decisively what is most beneficial for me.

The Supreme Personality of Godhead said: O sinless Arjuna, I have already explained that there are two classes of men who try to realize the Self. Some are inclined to understand it by factual, analytical speculation, and others by devotional service.

Not by merely abstaining from work can one achieve freedom from reaction, nor by renunciation (giving up) alone can one attain perfection.

Everyone is forced to act helplessly according to the qualities he has acquired from the modes of material nature; therefore no one can refrain from doing something, not even for a moment.

One who controls the senses of action but whose mind thinks on sense objects certainly misleads himself and is called a pretender.

On the other hand, if a sincere person tries to control the active senses by the mind and begins karma-yoga [in Krishna consciousness] without attachment, he is by far superior.

Perform your prescribed duty, for doing so is better than not working. One cannot even maintain one's physical body without work.

Work done as a sacrifice for Vishnu has to be performed; otherwise work causes bondage in this material world. Therefore, O son of Kunti, perform your prescribed duties for His satisfaction, and in that way you will always remain free from bondage.

In the beginning of creation, the Lord of all creatures sent forth generations of men and demigods, along with sacrifices for Vishnu, and blessed them by saying, "Be thou happy by this yajna [sacrifice] because its performance will bestow upon you everything desirable for living happily and achieving freedom."

The demigods, being pleased by sacrifices, will also please you, and thus, by cooperation between men and demigods, prosperity will reign for all.

In charge of the various necessities of life, the demigods, being satisfied by the performance of yajna [sacrifice], will supply all necessities to you. But he who enjoys such gifts without offering them to the demigods in return is certainly a thief.

The devotees of the Lord are released from all kinds of sins because they eat food that is offered first for sacrifice. Others, who prepare food for personal sense enjoyment, certainly eat only sin.

All living bodies survive on food grains, which are produced from rain. Rains are produced by performance of yajna [sacrifice], and yajna is born of prescribed duties.

Regulated activities are prescribed in the Vedas, and the Vedas are directly manifested from the Supreme Personality of Godhead. Consequently, the all-pervading Transcendence (Supremacy) is eternally situated in acts of sacrifice.

My dear Arjuna, one who does not follow in human life the cycle of sacrifice thus established by the Vedas certainly leads a life full of sin. Living only for the satisfaction of the senses, such a person lives in vain.

But for one who takes pleasure in the self, whose human life is one of self-realization, and who is satisfied in the self only, fully satiated— for him there is no duty.

A self-realized man has no purpose to fulfill in the discharge of his prescribed duties, nor has he any reason not to perform such work. Nor has he any need to depend on any other living being.

Therefore, without being attached to the fruits of activities, one should act as a matter of duty; for by working without attachment, one attains the Supreme.

Kings such as Janaka attained perfection solely by performance of prescribed duties. Therefore, just for the sake of educating the people in general, you should perform your work.

Whatever action a great man performs, common men follow. And whatever standards he sets by flawless acts, the entire world follows.

O son of Pritha, there is no work prescribed for Me within all the three planetary systems. Nor am I in want of anything, nor have I a need to obtain anything—and yet I am engaged in prescribed duties.

For if I ever failed to engage in carefully performing prescribed duties, O Partha, certainly all men would follow My path.

If I did not perform prescribed duties, all these worlds would be put to ruination. I would be the cause of creating unwanted population, and I would thereby destroy the peace of all living beings.

As the ignorant perform their duties with attachment to results, the learned may similarly act, but without attachment, for the sake of leading people on the right path.

So as not to disturb the minds of ignorant men attached to the fruitive results of prescribed duties, a learned person should not convince them to stop work. Rather, by working in the spirit of devotion, he should engage them in all sorts of activities [for the gradual development of Krishna consciousness].

The spirit soul confused by the influence of false ego thinks himself the doer of activities that are in actuality carried out by the three modes of material nature.

One who is in knowledge of the Absolute Truth, O mighty-armed, does not engage himself in the senses and sense pleasure, knowing well the differences between work in devotion and work for fruitive results.

Confused by the modes of material nature, the ignorant fully engage themselves in material activities and become attached. But the wise should not disturb them, although these duties are inferior due to the performers' lack of knowledge.

Therefore, O Arjuna, surrendering all your works unto Me, with full knowledge of Me, without desires for profit, with no claims to proprietorship, and free from lethargy, fight.

Those persons who executes their duties according to My instructions and who follows this teaching faithfully, without envy, become free from the bondage of fruitive actions.

But those who, out of envy, disregard these teachings and do not follow them are to be considered deprived of all knowledge, befooled, and ruined in their attempt for perfection.

Even a man of knowledge acts according to his own nature, for everyone follows the nature he has acquired from the three modes. What can suppression accomplish?

There are principles to regulate attachment and dislike pertaining to the senses and their objects. One should not come under the control of such attachment and dislike, because they are stumbling blocks on the path of self-realization.

It is far better to discharge one's prescribed duties, even though faultily, than another's duties perfectly. Destruction in the course of performing one's own duty is better than engaging in another's duties, for to follow another's path is dangerous.

Arjuna said: O descendant of Vrishni, by what is one compelled to sinful acts, even unwillingly, as if engaged by force?

The Supreme Personality of Godhead said: It is lust only, Arjuna, which is born of contact with the material mode of passion and later transformed into anger, and which is the all-consuming sinful enemy of this world.

As fire is covered by smoke, as a mirror is covered by dust, or as the embryo is covered by the womb, the living entity is similarly covered by different degrees of this lust.

Thus the wise living entity's pure consciousness becomes covered by his eternal enemy in the form of lust, which is never satisfied and which burns like fire.

The senses, the mind and the intelligence are the sitting places of this lust. Through them lust covers the real knowledge of the living entity and confuses him.

Therefore, O Arjuna, best of the Bharatas, in the very beginning curb this great symbol of sin [lust] by regulating the senses, and slay this destroyer of knowledge and self-realization.

The working senses are superior to dull matter; mind is higher than the senses; intelligence is still higher than the mind; and he [the soul] is even higher than the intelligence.

Thus knowing oneself to be transcendental (superior) to the material senses, mind and intelligence, O mighty-armed Arjuna, one should steady the mind by conscious spiritual intelligence [Krishna consciousness] and thus—by spiritual strength—conquer this unquenchable enemy known as lust.

Now let me Summarize Chapter 3:

Everyone is forced to act according to the qualities he has acquired by nature, so one should engage in some activity in this material world. Actions can either bind us to this world or liberate us from it. So one must perform their prescribed duty without attachment for fruitive results. Surrender all your work unto Lord Krishna without desiring for any profits. Thus by working for the Supreme Lord Krishna, without selfish motives is called Karma Yoga, one can become free from the law of karma (action and reaction) and attain transcendental (superior) knowledge of the self and the Supreme. Lord Krishna tells us that it is easy for people to follow the path of Karma

Yoga, the path of selfless service. Lord Krishna instructs Arjuna to do his duty and fight with knowledge and detachment. Lord Krishna also tells us that we must control our desire for sex pleasures, by keeping our mind steady and with spiritual intelligence [Krishna consciousness] conquer this uncontrollable enemy which lead us to failure and suffering in life.

I asked everyone, "Can anyone tell me what do you understand from this chapter?" One participant replied, "Lord Krishna instructs Arjuna to do his duty of a warrior and fight the war." The other said, "We must keep doing our duty without having any attachment to the results be it success or failure." One participant asked, "Madam you talked about Work life, please explain." I said, "The Bhagavad Gita has solution to every problem. Don't we face problems in our work life as well? We worry about success and failure. Managing relationships with bosses at work place is equally challenging. How many of you agree?" Everyone raised his or her hands. Here is a story of a woman who was harassed at her work place.

Do Your Duty

"Do your duty to the best of your ability, never give up and leave the rest to God".

There was a family of three, a husband wife and their five-year-old daughter. Both husband and wife were working professionals in top multinational companies in good positions. They were doing well for themselves; the husband and wife both had recently bought a beautiful house in a metropolitan city on loan. The wife was a beautiful lady and was making good progress in her company. Everything was going on great until one day.

One day, the wife's boss got transferred and she had to work with a new boss. This man started asking for sexual favors from this woman on pretext of promotion. The woman was very good at her work and refused his advances every time and on purpose she was not promoted. Unfortunately, this boss knew her husband's boss in the other company and he very tactfully played games to get her husband out of job so that his wife will agree to sleep with him. He played such wicked games that he could not get any job elsewhere. Only if she sleeps with him, not only will her husband get his job back but also this woman will get the much-deserved promotion along with increase in pay. But her boss had even more wicked plans, after sleeping with this woman he would send her to her husband's boss to sleep with him too.

There is a saying when bad luck comes it comes from everywhere. Unfortunately, their five-year-old daughter met with an accident and this woman urgently required leave from her company to attend to her daughter. Her boss again refused to give her leave and told her to stay and work or quit this job if you need to go to the hospital.

So, what will this woman do? She is stuck from all sides. Her job and pervert boss on one side, husband without job on the other side, home loan on the third side, her daughter in hospital on forth side and the prevailing threat to quit her job and if she quits her job she has no where to go, how will they survive?

She finally decided not to quit but to continue doing her duty. You won't believe something very interesting happened. The woman applied for an emergency leave and immediately left to attend to her daughter. After her daughter was all right and they came home from hospital, she filed a sexual harassment case against her boss without quitting her job, which was the right thing to do. After a legal battle of 6 months, she won and her husband also got his job back. Both the bosses lost their respective jobs reputation and got black listed from the employment market. This story tells us, one must keep doing their duty even if they are facing difficult circumstances or complex situations and in the mean time either try to improvise the matter, look for solutions or patiently look for better options. So do your duty to the best of your ability and leave the rest to God.

In 2008, the whole world was experiencing recession. It affected my life too. All my clients stopped giving business. There was no possibility of getting fresh business because of slow down. My funds got exhausted, my employees left. My investor refused to fund. I was in a state of hopelessness. No work, no employees, no money. What could I do? Close down. Give up. No, I decided to continue working without funds in my account. I decided to do my duty. After few months, market started opening up and slowly business got back to normal. In other words, I did my duty in a phase of hopelessness didn't give up and left the rest to God.

Once a trainer was teaching a batch of employees about how to overcome stress. The employees were happy to gain the insight and learning. But when the trainer enquired about their wellbeing after few months, the reaction was negative. The trainer felt sad and depressed that he failed to help people in need and he even thought of discontinuing his path of being a trainer. Later I encouraged him to continue doing his duty irrespective of success or failure, one shouldn't stop from doing work that he believes in, instead keep improvising from the feedback and leave the rest to God.

Mahatma Gandhi had said, "Gita is my Eternal Mother. I confess to you that, when doubts haunt me, when disappointments stare me in the face, and when I see not one ray of light on the horizon, I run to the Bhagavad Gita and find a verse to comfort me, and I immediately begin to smile in the midst of overwhelming sorrow." Gita, his Eternal Mother, showed him the way from darkness to eternal light, eternal truth and eternal bliss and advised him to do two things: First, to master the skill of action and second to remain balanced and equipoised in success or failure. He said, "Do your work as duty par excellence, but renounce the desire for the fruit of action."

In the Bhagavad Gita, when Arjuna was overcome by grief of having to kill his own blood relatives on the battlefield of Kurukshetra and he refused to fight and gave up. At that time, Lord Krishna reminded him of his duties as a Kshatriya and told him not to give up but to get up do his duty with a balanced mind and leave the results of war be it success or failure on Him. If you come across any hopeless situation, have you ever thought what would you do? Quitting and running away from problems in not the answer. Facing your problems and looking for solutions is the right thing to do. Mahatma Gandhi too followed the teaching of the Bhagavad Gita. Here is another important life lesson.

**Lesson No: 7 Do your duty to the best of your ability, even if there is hopelessness around. Never give up and leave the results be it success or failure on God.

One hand went up, it was Shikha. "Yes Shikha, any question?" She said, "How can we work when there are problems going on in our personal life?" Looking at Shikha I said, "That's what I told earlier, if one leg of that chair is broken we fall down, emotionally and physically. But the above story also says, keep on working to the best of your ability even if there is hopelessness around, never give up and leave the results be it success or failure on God. Even if we face problems in our personal life, keep moving doing your daily routine work instead of just sitting at home and lamenting on what happened. The more you move out, focus on doing your work, slowly your mind will stop giving importance to the thoughts which disturb you and will start focusing on thoughts which keep you happy and busy. Surrender your problems to God; He is there to take care of it. This reminds me of a famous dialogue of Shah Rukh Khan "Main Hoon Na". Everyone laughed.

Another participant said, "Madam most of us do not like the work we do, but just because we have a family to take care of and loans to pay we work come what may. How can we enjoy something that we don't like and still be productive?"

Let me share a story with all of you.

Find Your Own Way

One day a young boy around 17 years old was sitting near the riverfront. He was crying his heart out and his tears were filling up the river. Lord Vishnu whose home is underwater could hear him cry. Immediately Lord Vishnu disguised Himself as a teacher and went to see the boy. Lord Vishnu asked the boy, "My child I'm seeing you from a long time that you are crying. Please share your problems, let me see if I can help."

The young boy said, "Go away, nobody can help me, I am confused myself." Lord Vishnu again asked, "Confused about what?"

The young boy said, "I do not know what work I should do to make a living. I do not understand what career to choose. I am a lost person."

Lord Vishnu smiled and said, "Oh it's very simple to find out. But what do your parents say about it?"

The young boy said, "My parents are cool, they have left this burden of choosing my career on me. They say I need to find my own way and they shall respect my decision and encourage me."

Lord Vishnu said, "Your parents have done the right thing, instead of forcing their impressions of what is good for you, they have told you to make a choice."

Further Lord Vishnu said, "Can I share some tips with you?"

The boy said, "Go ahead."

Lord Vishnu said, "Ask yourself what are the things you want to do before you die?"

"What are the things you love to do, that makes you happy?"

"What are the things you want to do even if you do not get paid for it, will you still do it with full love and dedication?"

"What are your Strengths and Weaknesses, analyze what kind of Opportunities you may want to grab or can come across, what are the

Threats or something which you are not comfortable with or you don't want to compromise with?"

"Just imagine, what if God comes in front of you and ask you for your wishes what would it be? Not like everyone who asks for lots of wealth, but honestly think about the kind of work you would love to do so that you automatically achieve success and happiness."

"Ask yourself 100 times, what is my hidden talent I'm born with? Write down all the words that come to your mind and you will find your connection."

The boy felt peaceful and happy with the answer. He said, "What if I'm still confused or not sure if I'm right, then?

Lord Vishnu said, "My child, have patience, your parents are guiding angels sent by God. Listen to their advice if you feel directionless at any point. Listen to your inner voice and I'm sure you will make the right choice."

Boy said, "What if I fail to realize my passion then?"

Lord Vishnu said, "You may realize your passion in the very beginning at a young age, some realize in their middle age and some when they retire. But never loose hope. Keep doing your work by giving your 100% and one day you will find your way."

Boy said, "What if I realize my passion on day but also realize that I can't earn much from it, or it may take a huge amount of loan to get started, then what should I do?

Lord Vishnu said, "You can always continue doing the work which feeds your family and if you have the time devote part time to your passion this will give you pleasure and inner satisfaction. If you passion requires huge investment and risks you have two choices, either go for it or just forget it and keep doing your work."

The young boy hugged the Lord and said, "Thank you for guiding me."

Lord said, "Lord Krishna had also advised Arjuna on the battlefield of Kurukshetra, that he must get up and fight the war. Arjuna was born in a Kshatriya family and his dharma was to fight. He was a great warrior. Similarly, we too need to find the qualities we are born with and do our karma, prescribed duty with full dedication without having any attachments for the results and surrender your work to God." Here comes another important life lesson.

**Lesson No: 8 Find your own way by finding your true passion. Find your hidden talent. Follow your inner voice.

It was 12 and everyone was looking at their watch. "I know its 12, we will now have a short tea break and come back at 12.20 pm.

CHAPTER 4

Arjuna Listen To Your Inner Voice

Everyone was seated after coming back from a short tea break. "Now we shall play a game. Game name is 'I know you'. We are 24 participants; we will form groups of 2 each. One person in the group is for example 'A' and the other person is 'B'. 'A' will talk on anything he or she likes except about himself or herself, 'B' has to just listen and find out about how 'A' is as a person, you can make assumptions or presumptions. Am I clear?" Few hands were up who were still not clear. "Let me share an example. When a boy meets a girl for the first time, he generally picks up a cheesy line to start a conversation with that girl. "Hey I know you, I have seen you in a party or an event before. You study in so and so college right." Before he approaches her, he tries to assume something before hand just by looking at her, trying to know her. Similarly, you need to do some guesswork. Now form groups of 2 each and decide amongst yourself who will be A and who will be B. Time is 3 minutes. Once time is up, all the 'B's' will come forward and share their findings about all the 'A's'. Your time starts now."

After time was up, one person from each group came forward and shared their finding about the other. Some were right and some were wrong and some were really funny. "How was the game?" I asked. Everyone said, "Good". I said, "This game has an interesting connection with Chapter 4 of The Bhagavad Gita and you will find out soon."

"It's time to get started with Chapter 4 of The Bhagavad Gita. This chapter has 42 shlokas. I request each participant to read one shloka each that is translated in English." Everyone started reading one after the other.

Transcendental Knowledge

The Personality of Godhead, Lord Shri Krishna, said: I instructed this imperishable science of yoga to the sun-god, Vivasvan, and

Vivasvan instructed it to Manu, the father of mankind, and Manu in turn instructed it to Ikshvaku.

This supreme science was thus received through the chain of disciplic succession, and the saintly kings understood it in that way. But in course of time the succession was broken, and therefore the science as it is appears to be lost.

*That very ancient science of the relationship with the Supreme is today told by Me to you because you are My devotee as well as My friend and can therefore understand the *transcendental* (superior) mystery of this science.*

Arjuna said: The sun-god Vivasvan is senior by birth to You. How am I to understand that in the beginning You instructed this science to him?

The Personality of Godhead said: Many, many births both you and I have passed. I can remember all of them, but you cannot, O conqueror of the enemy!

Although I am unborn and My transcendental body never deteriorates, and although I am the Lord of all living entities, I still appear in every millennium in My original transcendental form.

Whenever and wherever there is a decline in religious practice, O descendant of Bharata, and a predominant rise of irreligion—at that time I descend Myself.

In order to deliver the religious and to destroy the criminals, as well as to reestablish the principles of religion, I Myself appear, millennium after millennium.

One who knows the transcendental nature of My appearance and activities does not, upon leaving the body, take his birth again in this material world, but attains My eternal abode, O Arjuna.

Being freed from attachment, fear and anger, being fully absorbed in Me and taking refuge in Me, many, many persons in the past became purified by knowledge of Me—and thus they all attained transcendental love for Me.

As all surrender unto Me, I reward them accordingly. Everyone follows My path in all respects, O son of Pritha.

Men in this world desire success in fruitive activities, and therefore they worship the demigods. Quickly, of course, men get results from fruitive work in this world.

According to the three modes of material nature and the work associated with them, the four divisions of human society are created by Me. And although I am the creator of this system, you should know that I am yet the non-doer, being unchangeable.

There is no work that affects Me; nor do I aspire for the fruits of action. One who understands this truth about Me also does not become entangled in the fruitive reactions of work.

All the liberated souls in ancient times acted with this understanding of My transcendental nature. Therefore, you should perform your duty, following in their footsteps.

Even the intelligent are confused in determining what is action and what is inaction. Now I shall explain to you what action is, knowing which you shall be free from all misfortune.

The complex state of action is very hard to understand. Therefore, one should know properly what action is, what forbidden action is, and what inaction is.

One who sees inaction in action, and action in inaction, is intelligent among men, and he is in the transcendental position, although engaged in all sorts of activities.

One is understood to be in full knowledge whose every attempt is free of desire for sense pleasure. He is said by sages to be a worker for whom the reactions of work have been burned up by the fire of perfect knowledge.

Abandoning all attachment to the results of his activities, ever satisfied and independent, he performs no fruitive action, although engaged in all kinds of undertakings.

Such a man of understanding acts with mind and intelligence perfectly controlled, gives up all sense of proprietorship over his possessions, and acts only for the bare necessities of life. Thus working, he is not affected by sinful reactions.

He who is satisfied with gain that comes of its own accord, who is free from duality and does not envy, who is steady both in success and failure, is never entangled, although performing actions.

The work of a man who is unattached to the modes of material nature and who is fully situated in transcendental knowledge merges entirely into transcendence.

A person who is fully absorbed in Krishna consciousness is sure to attain the spiritual kingdom because of his full contribution to spiritual activities, in which the accomplishment is perfect and that which is offered is of the same spiritual nature.

Some yogis perfectly worship the demigods by offering different sacrifices to them, and some offer sacrifices in the fire of the Supreme Brahman.

Some [the unadulterated brahmacharis] sacrifice the hearing process and the senses in the fire of mental control, and others [the regulated householders] sacrifice the objects of the senses in the fire of the senses.

Others who are interested in achieving self-realization through control of the mind and senses, offer the functions of all the senses, and of the life breath, as religious offering into the fire of the controlled mind.

Having accepted strict vows, some become enlightened by sacrificing their possessions, and others by performing severe austerities, by practicing the yoga of eightfold mysticism, or by studying the Vedas to advance in transcendental knowledge.

Still others, who are inclined to the process of breath restraint to remain in trance, practice by offering the movement of the outgoing breath into the incoming, and the incoming breath into the outgoing, and thus at last remain in trance, stopping all breathing. Others, restricting the eating process, offer the outgoing breath into itself, as a sacrifice.

All these performers who know the meaning of sacrifice become cleansed of sinful reaction, and, having tasted the nectar of the results of sacrifices, they advance toward the supreme eternal atmosphere.

O best of the Kuru dynasty, without sacrifice one can never live happily on this planet or in this life: what then of the next?

All these different types of sacrifice are approved by the Vedas, and all of them are born of different types of work. Knowing them as such, you will become free.

O chastiser of the enemy, the sacrifice performed in knowledge is better than the mere sacrifice of material possessions. After all, O son of Pritha, all sacrifices of work culminate in transcendental knowledge.

Just try to learn the truth by approaching a spiritual master. Inquire from him submissively and render service unto him. The self-realized souls can impart knowledge unto you because they have seen the truth.

Having obtained real knowledge from a self-realized soul, you will never fall again into such illusion, for by this knowledge you will see that all living beings are but part of the Supreme, or, in other words, that they are Mine.

Even if you are considered to be the most sinful of all sinners, when you are situated in the boat of transcendental knowledge you will be able to cross over the ocean of miseries.

As a blazing fire turns firewood to ashes, O Arjuna, so does the fire of knowledge burn to ashes all reactions to material activities.

In this world, there is nothing so magnificent and pure as transcendental knowledge. Such knowledge is the mature fruit of all mysticism. And one who has become accomplished in the practice of devotional service enjoys this knowledge within himself in due course of time.

A faithful man who is dedicated to transcendental knowledge and who controls his senses is eligible to achieve such knowledge, and having achieved it he quickly attains the supreme spiritual peace.

But ignorant and faithless persons who doubt the revealed scriptures do not attain God consciousness; they fall down. For the doubting soul there is happiness neither in this world nor in the next.

One who acts in devotional service, giving up the fruits of his actions, and whose doubts have been destroyed by transcendental knowledge, is situated firmly in the self. Thus he is not bound by the reactions of work, O conqueror of riches.

Therefore the doubts that have arisen in your heart out of ignorance should be slashed by the weapon of knowledge. Armed with yoga, O Bharata, stand and fight.

Now let me Summarize Chapter 4:

What is transcendental knowledge? It is the spiritual knowledge of the relationship between a soul and Supreme Lord. Such knowledge is the blessing or fruit of selfless devotional service (karma yoga) and one enjoys this knowledge within himself in due course of time.

Both selfless devotional service (karma yoga) and transcendental knowledge (Self-knowledge or Supreme knowledge) free the soul from the bondage of karma. The Lord gives transcendental knowledge to those who do selfless devotional service. Transcendental knowledge burns all our past karma and frees us from the wheel or cycles of birth and death.

A faithful man who controls his senses and mind, become free from attachment, fear, desire for sense pleasure and anger. He who gives up all the fruits of his actions and surrenders to Lord Krishna is eligible to receive this transcendental knowledge and having achieved it he quickly attains the supreme spiritual peace.

The Lord also explains the remote history of the Gita, the purpose and significance of His periodic descents to the material world and the necessity of approaching a guru, a realized teacher to understand this pure transcendental knowledge.

Transcendental (superior)= An experience which is superior, spiritual, extremely special, unusual beyond the practical experience of ordinary people and cannot be understood by ordinary reasoning.

I asked everyone, "Can anyone tell me what do you understand from this chapter?" One participant replied, "Transcendental knowledge is Supreme knowledge." The other said, "Madam I couldn't understand a thing, please explain."

I said, "Would you all like to hear something interesting that I spoke about earlier and I am sure it will help you understand better." Everyone nodded.

I Found Someone

"Who do you think is the main hero of the Hindi movie, 'Koi Mil Gaya'?

No, it's not Hrithik Roshan. It is Jadoo the alien friend.

Let me translate the movie name in English it means, 'I found someone'.

Even I found someone who is similar to the character Jadoo.

He is my best friend who is always there with me and He has solution to every problem. He has also saved my father's life.

Few years ago, my dad was having persistent cough for 2 years. After showing to many doctors, one doctor said, "Why don't you get his entire body profile done." And...and...and...our worst nightmare came true. My dad got diagnosed with cancer in his right kidney. My entire family along with my dad got devastated on hearing this bad news. I couldn't understand what to do. I just knew that we had to find the best cancer surgeon and get him operated to remove the infected kidney. I sat down in deep thought and prayed to God asking for help. Then a negative thought came, "Am I going to loose my dad forever?" Someone replied, "No, he is going to be just fine." Then I got a vision wherein I remembered meeting a cancer surgeon at my aunt's place many years back. Again, I heard Someone say, "Call your aunt, ask for help, that doctor will help your dad". I immediately met my aunt and that doctor. My dad was operated by the same doctor and today by God grace he is doing fine. This miracle happened just because of that Someone who guided me to the right doctor and saved my father's life.

I'm sure by now, you must be waiting to know who that Someone is. Let me share a story with you.

One day God decided to hide somewhere where no human can find Him. He thought of hiding deep into the ground. No that won't work. Then He thought of hiding to the bottom of the deepest ocean. No that's a bad idea. He also thought of hiding at the highest mountain peak of the world. No humans are My smartest creation they will find Me. After a lot of thinking God found a solution. He said, "**I will place myself inside the hearts of every human being, for they will never think to look there**". Yes that Someone is My Inner Voice. He is not only within me, He is within you too. If you believe in Him, trust Him, ask for help He will save you from life threatening situations just like how He saved my dad. He is the real Jadoo within each one of us.

Imagine if you forget your keys one day, how do you happen to find it? Who guides you? Just think about it. If you feel lost in your life who guides you to the right direction and to your true self that's your inner voice. The Phulwama attack that shook the heart of every Indian. This wouldn't have happened, if that terrorist had found his inner voice, listened and followed it. There would be no terrorism in this world if everyone listened to his or her inner voice. Today, I have found Someone that's My inner voice, It's time you find yours.

Lord Krishna told Arjuna in the Bhagavad Gita that the doubts that have come to you are because of ignorance. You must kill these doubts with the weapon of transcendental knowledge, stand up and fight the war. Similarly, everyday we also come across problems and doubts in our lives with respect to health, wealth, relationships, work. But what are we doing about it? Are we living our lives in peace, harmony and happiness? If the answer you get is "No". Then its time to look within and find Someone that's your inner voice who will guide you to the right answer.

Now I want you all to go back to the experience of the game we just played 'I know you'. Anyone who was playing 'B' in the group, can you introspect and let me know who told you those answers about A? Think about it. One participant replied, "It was my inner voice." Yes, you are right. Here comes the most important life lesson.

Lesson No: 9 Look within find your inner voice, your intuition, trust it, listen to it and follow it with complete faith.

One participant raised his hand and asked, "Madam in previous chapter it was mentioned that Arjuna surrenders to Lord Krishna and in this chapter also you mentioned in summary that when one surrenders to Lord Krishna one becomes eligible to this transcendental knowledge. I want to understand, what do you mean by surrender, how does one surrender to Lord Krishna?"

I said, "Let me share a story of a woman who also asked the same question.

Surrender

One evening after having a cup of tea, a young married woman was sitting alone in her balcony at home and watching people pass by. As she was thinking, tears rolled down her eyes. She had recently lost her job because she was not able to focus on her work. Both her parents were hospitalized and were facing serious health issues because of which she was regularly visiting doctors and hospital, as she was their only daughter. Her husband, whom she loved so much, was unhappy about their relationship that lacked time and affection and he wanted to divorce her. She was indeed facing lot of problems.

She didn't understand what to do, somehow she felt that some unknown force is making things difficult for her. Is it her stars or is it the time or is it something to do with her karmas?

As she was thinking deeply and crying, her mother-in-law and father-in-law came up to her and sat next to her. They knew that she is going through tough time. So her father-in-law told her, "My dear daughter in life sometimes things don't go as planned. We come across challenges and tough times. The only way to go about it is the face those challenges instead of blaming them on bad time, karmas or our stars. It's very important to stay calm and balanced in our mind, which will help us pass through life's toughest tests. So just accept this test and sit for this exam and be determined to come out with flying colors.

Imagine you have become a student again and suddenly announcement has been made of a surprise test today. You have to sit for the exam, which you cannot avoid and which you have not prepared for or studied. The subject to your surprise is "Life". How would you feel?

Immediately you start feeling stressed and full of anxiety. You start thinking and talking to yourself, "What are the questions going to be? What if I don't know the answers? Then what will happen?

Some give up and quit accepting their failure, some beg for help from others asking to copy answers---but what if everyone has a different question paper? Rest try to write whatever they know.

But do you know who will pass the test?

Only that student who writes the exam with a calm and balanced mind, submits and surrenders to God asking for His help and guidance and who can let go off his or her anxieties, worries and fear of success or failure of this exam. That student accepts whatever God decides because he or she trusts God and has firm faith in the Divine.

The young married woman stopped crying and asked her father-in-law, "Dad how can I surrender myself to God? How can I seek His help and guidance? How will I know what to do when I see problems coming from all directions?"

Father-in-law looked at his wife and the mother-in-law said, "My dear daughter let me share an interesting story of Lord Krishna with you.

One day a household man came to meet Lord Krishna at his palace in Dwarka. He wanted a favor from Lord. Lord Krishna asked, "Tell me how can I help you?" The household man said, "Lord please hang me to death. I don't want to live any longer, I am fed up of this life." Lord Krishna was surprised to hear this. He thought probably this man wants financial help like others. But on hearing this He was taken aback.

Lord Krishna asked, "But why do you want to die? What wrong did you do?"

The household man said, "Lord my son is born with disability he can neither walk nor talk, my wife has become depressed and insane, I am in deep financial debt. People talk ill about me because of my current condition, saying he must have done some bad deeds in his past lives."

"I know You are Lord of the Lords, if I beg You to relieve me from my sufferings You can and You might just use Your magical powers and make everything alright. But I also know You won't and can't go against the rules laid down by the Universe. I have to live with this suffering, which is written in my destiny. But Lord I just cannot continue, I don't want to live anymore. Please give me death sentence."

Lord Krishna said, "I must say you have understood life in the right way. But running away from problems is not the answer. The only way is to Surrender unto Me, let go off your fears of how you will live this life full of suffering. Learn to ignore what people say about you. Accepting however your life is and facing your challenges is the only way."

The household man asked, "But Lord how can I Surrender unto You? How can I learn to let go my fears, worries and anxiety? Today if I follow Your instructions, tomorrow again these negative thoughts will take over my mind. Today If I ignore what people are saying, tomorrow again they will say hurtful things and then again I will get into depression."

Lord Krishna said, "Surrender means giving yourself completely to Me. Ask for forgiveness from all your current, past and past lives bad deeds, which you must have done knowingly and unknowingly. Forgive those souls whom you must have hurt knowingly or unknowingly in your current, past or past lives. Forgive those souls who have hurt you in this life. Honest tears of forgiveness will flow through your eyes. When you surrender unto Me and ask for forgiveness, I give you shelter, help and guide. By doing this you will not only feel better from within, but you will gain inner strength and courage to face your struggles and challenges.

By My Grace, you will be able to hear your inner voice. It will guide you to do the right things and follow the right path. You just need to trust it and follow it blindly without asking questions.

When negative thoughts will haunt you, this inner voice will keep telling you what to do. This inner voice will guide you repeatedly to ignore things, people and situations beyond your control and think positive in every situation. You just need to stay calm and balanced in your mind."

The household man was dumbfounded. He Thanked Lord Krishna for His guidance and left the palace."

The young married woman smiled and thanked both her in laws for guiding her and supporting her in this phase of her life.

She then surrendered to Lord Krishna and practiced forgiveness. Very soon from a depressed lost soul she became a new confident person. She immediately gave her full attention and focus to her ailing parents. Her husband also came in to help her. With a calm mind she was able to identify the right doctor and treatment for her parents. Soon her parents got well and in this process her communication with her husband became good. Misunderstanding cleared and their relationship got back on track. After few months she dropped the idea of taking up a new job instead a new desire of becoming a mother came up and she very soon was blessed with a baby girl into her life.

On the battlefield of Kurukshetra, Lord Krishna told Arjuna to surrender unto Him. Lord Krishna told Arjuna, "Become free from attachment, fear and anger. Become fully absorbed in Me, take refuge in Me. Like many persons in the past you too will become purified by knowledge of Me and thus attain spiritual love for Me. As all surrender unto Me, I reward accordingly. Even if you are sinful of all sinners, when you are sitting on the boat of spiritual knowledge you will be able to cross over the oceans of miseries. Slash the doubts that have come to you out of ignorance by the weapon of spiritual knowledge. As a blazing fire turns firewood to ashes, O Arjuna, so does the fire of knowledge burn to ashes all reactions to material activities. Stand up and fight."

Here comes another life lesson.

**Lesson No: 10 Completely Surrender yourself to God. Through spiritual knowledge He will guide you and help you cross over the oceans of miseries.

CHAPTER 5

I Am Everywhere

It's time for some music. I played the song "*Tujh main Rab dikta hai*" from the Hindi movie "*Rab ne bana di Jodi*" starring Shah Rukh Khan and Anushka Sharma. When the music was playing I could see everyone had transported themselves back to their loved ones or exes. "How was the song?" I asked. Everyone said, "Very nice." One participant asked, "Does it have a connection with Chapter 5 of The Bhagavad Gita?" I said, "It seems you are still playing the game 'I know you' and you are right. We will talk about it as we proceed ahead."

"It's time to get started with Chapter 5 of The Bhagavad Gita. This chapter has 29 shlokas. I request each participant to read one shloka each that is translated in English." Everyone started reading one after the other.

Karma-yoga-Action in Krishna Consciousness

Arjuna said: O Krishna, first of all You ask me to renounce (give up) work, and then again You recommend work with devotion. Now will You kindly tell me definitely which of the two is more beneficial?

The Personality of Godhead replied: The renunciation of work and work in devotion are both good for freedom. But, of the two, work in devotional service is better than renunciation of work.

One who neither hates nor desires the fruits of his activities is known to be always renounced. Such a person, free from all dualities, easily overcomes material bondage and is completely liberated, O mighty-armed Arjuna.

Only the ignorant speak of devotional service [karma-yoga] as being different from the analytical study of the material world [Sankhya].

Those who are actually learned say that he who applies himself well to one of these paths achieves the results of both.

One who knows that the position reached by means of analytical study can also be attained by devotional service, and who therefore sees analytical study and devotional service to be on the same level, sees things as they are.

Merely renouncing all activities yet not engaging in the devotional service of the Lord cannot make one happy. But a thoughtful person engaged in devotional service can achieve the Supreme without delay.

One who works in devotion, who is a pure soul, and who controls his mind and senses is dear to everyone, and everyone is dear to him. Though always working, such a man is never entangled.

A person in the divine consciousness, although engaged in seeing, hearing, touching, smelling, eating, moving about, sleeping and breathing, always knows within himself that he actually does nothing at all. Because while speaking, evacuating, receiving, or opening or closing his eyes, he always knows that only the material senses are engaged with their objects and that he is aloof from them.

One who performs his duty without attachment, surrendering the results unto the Supreme God, is unaffected by sinful action, as the lotus leaf is untouched by water.

The yogis, abandoning attachment, act with body, mind, intelligence, and even with the senses, only for the purpose of purification.

The steadily devoted soul attains unadulterated peace because he offers the result of all activities to Me; whereas a person who is not in union with the Divine, who is greedy for the fruits of his labor, becomes entangled.

When the embodied living being controls his nature and mentally renounces all actions, he resides happily in the city of nine gates [the material body], neither working nor causing work to be done.

The embodied spirit, master of the city of his body, does not create activities, nor does he convince people to act, nor does he create the fruits of action. All this is enacted by the modes of material nature.

Nor does the Supreme Lord assume anyone's sinful or religious activities. Embodied beings, however, are confused because of the ignorance that covers their real knowledge.

When, however, one is enlightened with the knowledge by which ignorance is destroyed, then his knowledge reveals everything, as the sun lights up everything in the daytime.

When one's intelligence, mind, faith and refuge are all fixed in the Supreme, then one becomes fully cleansed of misgivings through complete knowledge and thus proceeds straight on the path of liberation.

The humble sages, by virtue of true knowledge, see with equal vision a learned and gentle brahmana, a cow, an elephant, a dog and a dog-eater [outcaste].

Those whose minds are established in sameness and calmness have already conquered the conditions of birth and death. They are flawless like Brahman, and thus they are already situated in Brahman.

A person who neither rejoices upon achieving something pleasant nor complains upon obtaining something unpleasant, who is self-intelligent, who is not confused, and who knows the science of God, is already situated in transcendence.

Such a liberated person is not attracted to material sense pleasure but is always in half-conscious state, enjoying the pleasure within. In this way the self-realized person enjoys unlimited happiness, for he concentrates on the Supreme.

An intelligent person does not take part in the sources of misery, which are due to contact with the material senses. O son of Kunti, such pleasures have a beginning and an end, and so the wise man does not delight in them.

Before giving up this present body, if one is able to tolerate the urges of the material senses and check the force of desire and anger, he is well situated and is happy in this world.

One whose happiness is within, who is active and rejoices within, and whose aim is inward is actually the perfect mystic. He is liberated in the Supreme, and ultimately he attains the Supreme.

Those who are beyond the dualities that arise from doubts, whose minds are engaged within, who are always busy working for the welfare of all living beings, and who are free from all sins achieve liberation in the Supreme.

Those who are free from anger and all material desires, who are self-realized, self-disciplined and constantly aiming for perfection, are assured of liberation in the Supreme in the very near future.

Shutting out all external sense objects, keeping the eyes and vision concentrated between the two eyebrows, suspending the inward and outward breaths within the nostrils—thus controlling the mind, senses and intelligence, the transcendentalist aiming at liberation becomes free from desire, fear and anger. One who is always in this state is certainly liberated.

A person in full consciousness of Me, knowing Me to be the ultimate beneficiary of all sacrifices and austerities, the Supreme Lord of all planets and demigods, and the helper and well-wisher of all living entities, attain peace from the pains of material miseries.

Now let me Summarize Chapter 5:

Arjuna asks Lord Krishna what is good, renounce (giving up) of work or work in devotion. Lord Krishna considers the path of devotional (selfless) service to humanity without attachment to its results as the best path for most people. Both paths, the path of self-knowledge and the path of devotional service, lead to a happy life here on the earth and after death. Sanyasa does not mean leaving worldly possessions. It means not being attached to them. The man even though physically performs all actions but from within gives up the fruits, gets purified by transcendental knowledge, attains peace, detachment, patience, spiritual vision and bliss. The one who is free from anger, doubts, material desires, who is self-realized, self-disciplined, who works for the welfare of all living beings and who is free from all sins achieves liberation. An enlightened person sees the Lord in all beings and treats everybody equally.

I asked everyone, "Can anyone tell me what do you understand from this chapter?" One participant replied, "It talks about two paths, the path of self-knowledge and the path of devotional service." The other said, "I was able to understand about Sanyasa."

I said, "Great findings. But this chapter teaches us something even more amazing thing and a very important lesson. Here is another interesting thing that I am going to share.

I Can See You, Feel You, Hear You

Swami Vivekananda once said, "The highest truth is: God is present in every being! There is no other God to seek for! He alone is worshipping God, who serves all beings!" God is present in each one of us, in every being— be it human, animal, beggars, saints, holy men, friends and enemies, etc. God is present everywhere.

One day I had gone for a client meeting to an IT park. The meeting was at 4pm. When I reached the gate the security guard told me to park my car outside on the road opposite to the gate. As mine was visitor's car, according to their policy outside cars were not allowed. I found parking outside and parked my car and went for the meeting. After an hour or so I came out of the meeting and was about to leave. As the parking was full, I thought of taking a little reverse and then move ahead. As it was evening 5pm the sun was setting behind I couldn't see that there was a big hole and my car's one rear tyre went into the hole. I felt something has gone wrong and I came out of the car to see it. To my shock, my car's rear tyre was stuck in the hole and little ahead of the hole about 1000 feet was dug up for construction. I got scared and asked God to help me, didn't understand what to do. Immediately a rickshaw driver came to my rescue and instructed me to give the right pressure on the accelerator that will take the rear wheel out of the hole. If I made any mistake, my car along with me can go down 1000 feet and I'm dead. I did escape that dreadful moment and thanked the rickshaw driver for saving my life. God did come to help in the form of rickshaw driver.

We should never expect God to come directly and help us, he will send someone or He will come in any form to help. We should see God in all and help others and make them happy then God will be pleased by us because we are indirectly making Him happy. So proudly say, I can see You.

Few years back, one of my friends was looking for a life partner and was meeting different proposals for marriage. One day, she planned to meet one guy whom she liked on phone and his overall profile on one of the matrimonial sites. In today's times the guy and girl feel that they want to first meet, decide and then let their parents take this further. That day the girl was waiting for the guy; they were going to meet at a coffee shop. The moment the guy appeared and they met, she got some very weird, bad vibrations or feelings about this guy. She couldn't understand what was going on and ignored it. She then continued having coffee and conversations with him. Their dating continued and she got friendly with him. After few days, this guy started asking about her previous relationships and the girl told him all about her past. Somehow the guy didn't like the girl's past history and he decided to move away, but not like that. He had some dangerous plan in mind. He invited her for dinner one day. That night, he took her to outskirts of the city there he drank a lot at his friend's place then went on to have dinner at a restaurant with the girl. Post dinner, on repeatedly insisting by the girl to go back, he stopped the car and started molesting her. The girl got scared and threatened to shout and run away, but he paid no heed to her. Then he drove his car in the opposite direction and took her to a lodge nearby and raped her. She was shattered and devastated with how the events turned up side down. Repeatedly on pleading the guy left her home and she vowed never to see that bastard again. The girl didn't report her case to the police out of family prestige and kept quite. But this incident, completely changed her from an outspoken person to an introvert, she lost her confidence and went into depression. But this incident taught her a big lesson, to listen and respect the unknown vibrations that communicate with us and warn us to stay away. This unknown energy is none other than God communicating with us. So, now you know that God is present everywhere, I can feel You.

One day a young man was standing outside a temple. People were looking at him with surprise as to why is he standing outside the temple and not going in. The priest of the temple even asked him, "What happened my child why are you not entering the temple of God, don't you believe in God?" The young man said, "I truly believe in God, but I want to find God." The priest smiled and said, "Then you do one thing, travel to any place whichever you like or the place you have been waiting to go in a long time but travel all alone." The young man was puzzled and asked, "Why alone?" The priest said, "Just go, you will find what you are looking for."

The young man actually planned and went on a trip alone. He had never travelled alone before but thought it will be a good experience to travel to his most awaited destination. The scenic beauty, natural landscape, amazing weather just kept him wanting for more. The local food and courteous people made him feel happy. As he was walking on the beach, he was witnessing God's abundance gifted to mankind that is Mother Nature. He couldn't feel the stress that he used to experience when he was working.

No worries, no anxiety, only relaxation, peace and calmness. Suddenly, he heard a voice saying to him, "Hi young man, are you looking for Me?" With surprise he looks around to find who is talking to him. He cannot see anyone. Then he continued his walk. Again he heard the same voice, "Hey I'm here, I am happy to know that you wanted to meet Me." He again couldn't see anyone, he thought hope no ghost is following him. Again he heard the same voice. Oh! the young man was shocked to know. This beautiful voice was coming from nowhere else but from within him. He was surprised for a moment and then started talking with God. He experienced the happiest moment of his life and felt peace and calm. The priest did guide him rightly. God is in all of us and in the external world. God is everywhere. When our desire to find God becomes strong, the God within us awakes & shows us His way. So, now you can say boldly I can hear You.

On the battlefield of Kurukshetra, Lord Krishna told Arjuna that the humble wise person is one who by virtue of true knowledge can see with equal vision a learned and gentle Brahmin, a cow, an elephant, a dog and an animal-eater. An enlightened person sees Me in all beings and treats everybody equally. When you serve all beings you worship Me directly. So now you can see Me, feel Me and hear Me.

Coming to the point of that beautiful Hindi song, 'Tujh main Rab dikta hai', it says everything. When we start seeing God in everyone, then we become truly enlightened beings. That's why it becomes even more important that we start helping others in need. Whenever we see anyone injured in an accident immediately help that person in need. He or she needs your help and not the Yamraj, God of death. Whenever you face any trouble in your relationships, just sing this beautiful song to your loved one and see how magically your anger, frustration and anxiety wipes off. Believe that God is in everyone and everywhere and then you will be able to truly see Him, feel Him and hear Him. Here comes the most important life lesson.

Lesson No: 11 God is present everywhere. You can see Him in all beings, so help everyone. You can feel Him, learn to trust your inner vibrations. You can hear Him, listen to your inner voice.

As expected Shikha's hand was up, "Yes Shikha, you can ask me a question." She said, "In one story, you thank the rickshaw driver to save your life and considered him as form of God and in other story that man molested the woman on pretext of marriage, how can we think of such a monster as God?" I said, "You are right, we cannot think of such a monster as God, as human beings we differentiate that person based on his actions. But God doesn't differentiate between them. He is indeed residing in each one of us; the only difference lies is in our awareness and belief. Where one person becomes enlightened by becoming aware of God presence within him or her and believes in God, the other is ignorant and acts according to his nature. That is why it becomes important to trust our vibrations."

Another participant raises his hand and says, "In today's times, everyone is selfish and materialistic, how can we motivate ourselves and encourage others to help each other." I said, "For that let me share an interesting story.

The Businessman

Once a businessman started his own venture by borrowing money from his friends and by putting his savings. After few years into business, he felt the heat of competitors growing and market demand changing rapidly. With time his business started showing a downturn. He had to do something very fast else his dream venture would collapse.

In deep thoughts his legs automatically took him to Lord Krishna's temple?

He sat there and started praying to Lord Krishna asking for help. After praying he felt such calm and peace that he dozed off in the temple.

That businessman then got a dream and Lord Krishna appeared and told him, "Start helping others and you will get everything you want." Now this businessman questioned Lord Krishna in turn by asking, "Lord if I will keep on solving others problems and keep helping others my business will get affected. In today's world, who has time to help or even think of others? If I invest time in helping, I will not be able to devote time completely to my work and will loose business in turn. Please guide me."

Lord Krishna smiled and said, "Just trust Me and do as I say. Help others from your heart without any expectation and don't worry about anything else. At the same time keep working instead of worrying."

Then immediately the businessman woke up, thanked Lord Krishna for guiding him and left.

The businessman religiously did as he was told. Instead of worrying about his work, he gave 100% to his work and also started helping others without any expectations. Slowly the ones whom he helped became his goodwill ambassadors and they started spreading his name in the market. He became famous in his business circle and his hands were always full of work. That was indeed his success mantra.

When you choose and take a step forward to help others from all your heart without any expectations, blessings in the form of wealth, peace and success automatically enter your life. In today's times, if everyone starts thinking of helping others, I'm sure we will be living in a better place and live a more peaceful and happy life. So if the saying is true that, "God helps those who help themselves", then this also holds true that, "God blesses those who helps others."

Lord Krishna explains Arjuna that he should consider the path of devotional (selfless) service to humanity without having any attachment to its results as the best path. Just by giving up (renouncing) his duties, as a warrior and not fighting, will not do any good to him. Lord Krishna says, "One who performs his duty without attachment, surrendering the results unto the Supreme God, is unaffected by sinful action, as the lotus leaf is untouched by water. The steadily devoted soul attains peace because he offers the result of all activities to Me; whereas a person who is not in union with the Divine, who is greedy for the fruits of his labor, becomes entangled."

This explains us why the path of devotional (selfless) service to humanity is the best path and helping others is not time consuming but time worth investing. Here comes another life lesson.

Lesson No: 12 Think of the pain and needs of others and work to help them. This is secret formula to achieve happiness and success in life.

It's now time for lunch. I'm sure you all must be very hungry by now. Time now is 1.30 pm and we all will gather again at 2.30 pm."

CHAPTER 6

Meditation

"How was the lunch?" I asked. Everyone said, "Delicious, good, amazing." I said, "Great now let's continue. One day I had a flight to take to New Delhi at 10am. It so happened that my alarm rang rang rang on time but I was still sleeping, as the ringer of the alarm was kept by mistake on a low volume. I woke up at 6am. I immediately started to worry on getting late. I somehow managed to pack and get ready. Then the taxi guy was late, I got frustrated because the airport was at a 1-hour distance from my place. On my way I got stuck in traffic just outside the airport. When I reached the check in counter, it just got closed a minute before. I got furious and angry not on the airline staff but on myself. I request and begged her to check me in, but their system just doesn't permit to do so. I was feeling very angry, frustrated, confused, moving from one corner to other. Stop, sit down, calm down. Take control of your breathing. From heavy breathing move to breathing slowly, breathe in breathe out, breathe in breathe out. Relax. I have just meditated in my most negative state. Immediately my name was announced, and they let me in. I'm sure we all have experienced negativity many a times. If someone says something to you immediately negative thoughts start flooding our mind one after the other. If our day starts on a bad note, the entire day we face events or people with bad taste. What can we do about it? How can we change or take charge of our negative mood and change it to positivity?

First thing to do is become aware of the negative energy within us.

Second thing is to meditate by taking control of our breathing.

Meditation is the best way to take charge of your emotions."

"Chapter 6 of The Bhagavad Gita is about Dhyana Yoga that is nothing but Meditation. This chapter has 47 shlokas. I request each participant to read one shloka each that is translated in English." Everyone started reading one after the other.

Dhyana-yoga

The Supreme Personality of Godhead said: One who is unattached to the fruits of his work and who works as he is committed is in the renounced order of life, and he is the true mystic, not he who lights no fire and performs no work.

What is called renunciation you should know to be the same as yoga, or linking oneself with the Supreme, O son of Pandu, for one can never become a yogi unless he renounces the desire for sense pleasure.

For one who is a beginner in the eightfold yoga system, work is said to be the means; and for one who is already elevated in yoga, ending of all material activities is said to be the means.

A person is said to be elevated in yoga when, having renounced all material desires, he neither acts for sense pleasure nor engages in fruitive activities.

One must deliver himself with the help of his mind, and not degrade himself. The mind is the friend of the conditioned soul, and his enemy as well.

For him who has conquered the mind, the mind is the best of friends; but for one who has failed to do so, his mind will remain the greatest enemy.

For one who has conquered the mind, the Supersoul is already reached, for he has attained peace. To such a man happiness and distress, heat and cold, honor and dishonor are all the same.

A person is said to be established in self-realization and is called a yogi [or mystic] when he is fully satisfied by virtue of acquired knowledge and realization. Such a person is situated in transcendence and is self-controlled. He sees everything—whether it be pebbles, stones or gold—as the same.

A person is considered still further advanced when he regards honest well-wishers, affectionate helpers, the neutral, mediators, the envious, friends and enemies, the religious and the sinners all with an equal mind.

A transcendentalist should always engage his body, mind and self in relationship with the Supreme; he should live alone in a secluded place and should always carefully control his mind. He should be free from desires and feelings of possessiveness.

To practice yoga, one should go to a secluded place and should lay kusa grass on the ground and then cover it with a deerskin and a soft cloth. The seat should neither be too high nor too low and should be situated in a sacred place. The yogi should then sit on it very firmly and practice yoga to purify the heart by controlling his mind, senses and activities and fixing the mind on one point.

One should hold one's body, neck and head erect in a straight line and stare steadily at the tip of the nose. Thus, without being physically and mentally disturbed, with a quiet mind, without fear, completely free from sex life, one should meditate upon Me within the heart and make Me the ultimate goal of life.

Thus practicing constant control of the body, mind and activities, the mystic transcendentalist, his mind regulated, attains to the kingdom of God [or the abode of Krishna] by end of material existence.

There is no possibility of one's becoming a yogi, O Arjuna, if one eats too much or eats too little, sleeps too much or does not sleep enough.

He who is regulated in his habits of eating, sleeping, recreation and work can lessen all material pains by practicing the yoga system.

When the yogi, by practice of yoga, disciplines his mental activities and becomes situated in transcendence—free of all material desires— he is said to be well established in yoga.

As a lamp in a windless place does not waver, so the transcendentalist, whose mind is controlled, remains always steady in his meditation on the transcendent self.

In the stage of perfection called trance, or samadhi, one's mind is completely controlled from material mental activities by practice of yoga. This perfection is characterized by one's ability to see the self by the pure mind and to relish and rejoice in the self. In that joyous state, one is situated in boundless transcendental happiness, realized through transcendental senses. Established thus, one never departs from the truth, and upon gaining this he thinks there is no greater gain. Being situated in such a position, one is never shaken, even in *the midst of greatest difficulty. This indeed is actual freedom from all miseries arising from material contact.*

One should engage oneself in the practice of yoga with determination and faith and not be deviated from the path. One should abandon, without exception, all material desires born of mental speculation and thus control all the senses on all sides by the mind.

Gradually, step-by-step, one should become situated in trance by means of intelligence sustained by full conviction, and thus the mind should be fixed on the self-alone and should think of nothing else.

From wherever the mind wanders due to its flickering and unsteady nature, one must certainly withdraw it and bring it back under the control of the self.

The yogi whose mind is fixed on Me certainly attains the highest perfection of transcendental happiness. He is beyond the mode of passion, he realizes his qualitative identity with the Supreme, and thus he is freed from all reactions to past deeds.

Thus, the self-controlled yogi, constantly engaged in yoga practice, becomes free from all material contamination and achieves the highest stage of perfect happiness in transcendental loving service to the Lord.

A true yogi observes Me in all beings and also sees every being in Me. Indeed, the self-realized person sees Me, the same Supreme Lord, everywhere.

For one who sees Me everywhere and sees everything in Me, I am never lost, nor is he ever lost to Me.

Such a yogi, who engages in the worshipful service of the Supersoul, knowing that I and the Supersoul are one, remains always in Me in all circumstances.

He is a perfect yogi who, by comparison to his own self, sees the true equality of all beings, in both their happiness and their distress, O Arjuna!

Arjuna said: O Madhusudana, the system of yoga that You have summarized appears impractical and unacceptable to me, for the mind is restless and unsteady.

The mind is restless, unstable, stubborn and very strong, O Krishna, and to master it, I think, is more difficult than controlling the wind.

Lord Shri Krishna said: O mighty-armed son of Kunti, it is undoubtedly very difficult to curb the restless mind, but it is possible by suitable practice and by detachment.

For one whose mind is uncontrolled, self-realization is difficult work. But he whose mind is controlled and who tries hard by appropriate means is assured of success. That is My opinion.

Arjuna said: O Krishna, What is the destination of the unsuccessful transcendentalist, who in the beginning takes to the process of self-realization with faith but who later stops doing it due to worldly-mindedness and thus does not attain perfection in mysticism?

O mighty-armed Krishna, does not such a man, who is confused from the path of transcendence, fall away from both spiritual and material success and perish like a split cloud, with no position in any sphere?

This is my doubt, O Krishna, and I ask You to eliminate it completely. But for You, no one is to be found who can destroy this doubt.

The Supreme Personality of Godhead said: Son of Pritha, a transcendentalist engaged in auspicious activities does not meet with destruction either in this world or in the spiritual world; one who does good, My friend, is never overcome by evil.

The unsuccessful yogi, after many, many years of enjoyment on the planets of the religious living entities, is born into a family of righteous people, or into a family of rich aristocracy.

Or [if unsuccessful after long practice of yoga] he takes his birth in a family of transcendentalists who are surely great in wisdom. Certainly, such a birth is rare in this world.

On taking such a birth, he revives the divine consciousness of his previous life, and he again tries to make further progress in order to achieve complete success, O son of Kuru.

By goodness of the divine consciousness of his previous life, he automatically becomes attracted to the yogic principles—even without seeking them. Such an inquisitive transcendentalist stands always above the ritualistic principles of the scriptures.

And when the yogi engages himself with sincere attempt in making further progress, being washed of all contaminations, then ultimately, achieving perfection after many, many births of practice, he attains the supreme goal.

A yogi is greater than the ascetic, greater than the empiricist and greater than the fruitive worker. Therefore, O Arjuna, in all circumstances, be a yogi.

And of all yogis, the one with great faith who always acts in accordance with Me, thinks of Me within himself, and renders transcendental loving service to Me--he is the most intimately united with Me in yoga and is the highest of all. That is my opinion.

Now let me Summarize Chapter 6:

In Dhyana yoga Lord Krishna explains the very nature of the mind and how one can control the mind and the senses and focus concentration on Paramatma (the Supersoul, the form of the Lord situated in the heart). This is known as yoga, this practice culminates in samadhi, full consciousness of the Supreme. A true yogi sees Lord in all beings and also sees every being in Lord. The self-realized person sees the same Supreme Lord, everywhere.

However, Arjuna points out the main difficulty in practicing yoga is controlling the mind. Arjuna knows the restless, unsteady, strong nature of his mind and expresses his inability to practice this system of yoga. To which the Lord Krishna answers saying that it requires constant practice and detachment. The mind is most difficult to control and one has to conquer it otherwise lust, anger, illusion, etc. will deviate him. A conqueror of mind automatically follows dictation of Supersoul. Lord Krishna also tells about the destination of the unsuccessful yogi, who will take birth in a family of wise transcendentalists and automatically become attracted to yogic principles.

I asked everyone, "Can anyone tell me what do you understand from this chapter?" One participant replied, "It talks about the nature of the mind." The other said, "I was able to connect to my basic understanding of meditation." Another participant asked, "But how can I connect with Paramatma (the Supersoul) situated in my heart? Is the connection realized by the privileged few like the great saints or can a common person like me connect with the Paramatma within me?

I said, "What a beautiful question? Let me answer it."

Be Aware, Breathe And Listen

Prayer is talking to God, Meditation is listening to God.

Someone once asked Buddha, "What have you gained from meditation?" He said, "Nothing, but I lost anger, anxiety, depression, insecurity, fear, jealously."

Many years back, on a Sunday afternoon there were some unusual guests who came home. They didn't come from the main door, but they came to my balcony. They had two hands and two legs, and were making grunting and screeching sounds. Any guess, who were they? Yes, they were a group of 16 monkeys who were holidaying at my society enjoying their Sunday. My grandmother, who was enjoying a pleasant afternoon, happened to call me. She said, "Just observe these monkeys and tell me what do you see?" I told my grandmother, "They are bunch of useless creatures, jumping from one branch to another and they just cannot sit in one place." My grandmother smiled and said, "Do you know this is exactly the nature of our mind which is similar to a monkey that likes to wander and jumps from one thought to another. It likes to constantly swing between the past and the future. If you want to achieve success in life, you need to learn to tame this monkey mind." I asked, "But grandmother how can I control it?" Grandmother said, "You can control it with meditation." "But grandmother, what's that?" I enquired. Grandmother said, "When you give the monkey a banana to eat, what happens? He gets busy in the process of peeling and eating. Similarly, whenever our mind wanders we need to practice meditation to keep our mind clutter free, which makes us more focused and helps to hear our inner voice. The quieter you become the more you can hear." When we learn to control our monkey mind, we start becoming more aware of our breath and then can listen to the divine within.

Sometime back I came across this story from the book "Meditation by Osho". Once a man went to a saint. He said to him, "I am suffering from chain smoking for thirty years. I have fallen ill and doctors have given me a final warning to quit smoking or I will never be healthy. I have tried many times to quit but the urge is so much that I just cannot resist and fall into the same pattern again and again. Please help me." Saint said, "Thirty years is a long time and smoking has become your habit. Do one thing, forget about stopping. Just become aware whenever you smoke. This is called Smoking meditation." The man was shocked he said, "What are you saying? Are you crazy or something?" The Saint said, "Try it you have nothing to loose." The man said, "Ok, tell me." The Saint said, "Do one thing. When you are taking the packet of cigarettes out of your pocket, move slowly. Be conscious, alert, and aware; take it out slowly with full awareness, slowly not in old hurried way or unconscious way. Then start tapping the cigarette on your packet very alertly. Listen to the tapping sound, smell the cigarette, see its beautiful packing. Then put it in your mouth slowly, with full awareness, light it with full awareness. Enjoy every puff, become more and more aware. Then release the smoke, relax, another puff, go very slowly."

"If you can do it, you will be surprised; to see the whole stupidity of it. You will see it. Your inner voice will shout at you from within every time you take that puff. And then one day, you will quit. If you quit, great, but if you continue you need not worry about it." After three months the man came to see the saint and said, "Thank you I quit smoking." The saint said, "Great, now try with other things too. You have now learnt to de-automatize. You can overcome any bad habits with this meditation. With this method you can help others to quit drugs addiction, alcohol addiction and many more." Become more aware of your body, your urges, your addictions, breathe slowly to take control of it and listen to your inner voice.

Imagine you have found a magic lamp and it says, "Rub me and I shall deliver all the answers to your questions." In reality this can actually happen only when you learn to ignite your inner lamp with the help of meditation. For that you need to follow certain guidelines to achieve it. It's time for some practical session. Firstly, switch yourself off completely from day to day activities, keep your mobile phones on silent mode and just relax for some time. You can choose to relax lying on the bed or couch or any comfortable sitting position. Right now, we shall practice it here, later yoga trainer will have a similar session with you again. You need to find a place where there is silence and you can be alone. Choose anytime of the day, for 30 minutes. Now I request everyone to close their eyes. Take a deep breath, relax your entire body. We shall now start by focusing on your feet, move your feet clockwise then anticlockwise, relax and feel it getting relaxed. Then move on to your legs, relax and feel it getting relaxed. Then move to your thighs, relax and feel it getting relaxed. Then move to your abdomen, relax and feel it getting relaxed. Then move to your chest, relax and feel it getting relaxed. Then move on to your hands, relax and feel it getting relaxed. Then move on to your arms, relax and feel it getting relaxed. Then move on to your neck, turn it left to right, relax and feel it getting relaxed. Then move to your face, relax and feel it getting relaxed. Then move to your eyes, relax and feel it getting relaxed. Then move on to your eyebrows, relax and feel it getting relaxed. Then move on to your head, relax and feel it getting relaxed. Then move on to your brain, relax and feel it getting relaxed. Once you are in the relax mode, start focusing on your breathing. Place your one hand on your abdomen. When you breathe in, your stomach should move out, feel your stomach move out. When you breathe out, your stomach should move in, feel your stomach move in. Breathe in stomach out, breathe out stomach in, breathe in breathe out. Keep your focus on your breathing. Be alert and aware of your breathing. After breathing for 8-10 times, your mind will wander from one thought to another. Become aware of your thoughts. Thoughts will come like where are we going today for sightseeing, my project is still pending, my boss will kill me if I don't submit it by so and so deadline so on…Witness your thoughts as if like you are watching a movie within you. The moment you realize you are meditating, immediately move your focus from your wandering thoughts to your breathing process. Breathe in breathe out. Continue this process for sometime. Breathe in breathe out. Feel the calmness. Feel the stillness. Relax. You can open your eyes. I could see some participants sleeping to glory, snoring to glory. How did you all feel? Everyone said, "Relaxed, peaceful, nice, calm, rejuvenating." One participant said, "I felt so relaxed that I dozed off." I said, "No worries, It happens even you all had good lunch so dozing off is quite natural for few." Remember Meditate to recharge yourself. Practice this meditation technique everyday or whenever feasible on regular basis.

You must be wondering what about the magic lamp and the answers to your queries. Well, for that, after being consistent with the practice of meditation technique, you become eligible to ask any question to your Higher consciousness. Just one question at one time. And wait for the answer to come. Your inner voice will tell you how to go about it, what you should do. You can further have a question and answer session with respect to that topic. Like once I asked my Higher or Super consciousness, "God I am not keeping well, what should I do?" Do you know what answer I got? "Sheetal you are an idiot, when you know there is some problem within your body and it is not normal, you must quickly show yourself to a doctor without any further delay." We all do this mistake of not listening to our body and ignore pains and land up paying a bigger price after a long time. I got myself checked, got some tests done and finally after 2 years my problem got sorted out. Thanks to my inner voice and to the doctor who guided me in the right direction. Become more aware of your breath, by breathing from our stomach you will be able to hear your inner voice talking to you.

One participant then asked me, "Why breathe from stomach?" I said, "Have you seen a baby? How does the baby breathe? The baby breathes through the stomach. That's the reason why they are always in a happy state. Globally 500 million people meditate in different ways. Breathing meditation is also known as Vipassana and can de done sitting, walking and lying down."

For many years, I was doing meditation and was listening to my inner voice, but I had no idea that it was God speaking with me directly. It took me a lot of time to know, understand and trust it. An interesting meme that I came across, 'You relax in an airplane though you do not know the pilot, you relax in a ship though you do not know the captain, you relax in a train though you do not know the motorman, you relax in a bus though you do not know the driver, then why don't you relax in your life when you know that God is its controller? Trust your Lord. He is the Best Planner.' To know what has He planned for you "Meditate".

Lord Krishna also guided Arjuna to become a yogi, by telling him to conquer his mind, as the mind is the best of friends, but if he fails to do so, the mind will remain the greatest enemy. For one who has conquered the mind, the Supersoul is already reached and he has attained peace. To such a man happiness and distress, heat and cold, honor and dishonor are all the same. As a lamp in a windless place does not waver, so the transcendentalist, whose mind is controlled, remains always steady in his meditation on the transcendent self. To meditate, take control of your monkey mind, become aware of your body and breathe from your stomach, listen and trust "The Divine within you." Here is an important must follow life lesson.

**Lesson No: 13 Control your monkey mind through Meditation. Be aware of your body by becoming a Witness. Breathe from your stomach and learn to focus. Listen and Trust your inner voice.

One participant asked me, "Why do we need to practice meditation in solitude, where there is silence? As you did at the airport, can we not just do it anywhere anytime?" Another participant raised his hand and said, "My question is out of the blue, I just visualized the divine image of Lord Vishnu, why are most of his pictures in lying down and relaxed state?"

I said, "As for every problem there is a solution, to answer your question there is a story to tell."

Silence And Solitude

One day Narad Muni went to see Lord Vishnu. "Narayan! Narayan!" Lord Vishnu was as usual in his deep meditative state and He opened his eyes to talk with Narad Muni.

"How can I help you? What is your purpose of visiting me?" said Lord Vishnu.

Narad Muni said, "I have a question in my mind for a long time, thought of asking You today?" Lord Vishnu asked, "What is it, go ahead ask Me."

Narad Muni said, "Whenever I visit You, most of the times You are in a deep meditative relaxed state, I don't understand why?"

Lord Vishnu smiled and said, "This is exactly the state in which I meet my devotees."

Narad Muni replied, "I still haven't understood properly what You are trying to say."

Lord Vishnu further said, "This is called meditation. I meet my devotees one on one in this state. It is also called dhyana yoga. My devotees need to be disciplined in experiencing silence and calmness within themselves in a solitude place and after a lot of practice and patience they will experience Me within themselves."

Narad Muni quickly enquired, "Why silence and solitude?"

"Silence will free them from the external noise of the mind or the consciousness and will allow them to listen to their inner voice, that's My voice. Solitude will help them to connect with Me one on one," said the Lord.

Narad Muni said, "But Lord Vishnu, why would humans from today's times, that's Kaliyug, who lack patience and persistence, do meditation? In earlier times or yugs humans used to do extreme tapasya or austerities to impress You and would seek a boon."

Lord said, "In Satyayug, the fight was between two worlds (Devalok & Asuralok). Asuralok being the evil, was a different world.

In Tretayug, the fight was between Rama and Ravana. Both rulers were from two different countries.

In Dwaparayug, the fight was between Pandavas and Kauravas. Both good and evil were from the same family.

Kindly note how the evil is getting closer. From a different world to a different country to the same family. Now, do you know where is the evil in Kaliyug?

It is inside us. Both good and evil live within. The battle is within us. Who will the humans give victory to, their inner goodness or the evil within?

So the solution also lies within. The answer to that is meditation."

In the Bhagavad Gita, Arjuna mentioned to Lord Krishna that the mind is restless, unstable, stubborn and very strong it's very difficult to control it. The meditation Lord Krishna was talking about seemed impractical to Arjuna. Lord Krishna then said to Arjuna that He totally agrees with him, but one can control the mind with constant practice and detachment. Here is the life lesson to keep in mind.

Lesson No: 14 Meditation is the only one stop solution to all our problems. One can achieve the meditative state by constant practice of controlling the restless mind and detachment from external noisy consciousness. Practice mediation daily in silence and solitude.

CHAPTER 7

Arjuna Why Fear?

"I request everyone to write down your fears in the notepad. Time is 2 minutes." Everyone was looking at each other's faces. "If anyone is comfortable to share their fears, please stand up and say it." One participant said, "I am afraid of death", the other said, "I am afraid of getting killed in a bomb blast by terrorists." Yet another said, "I am afraid of ghosts." One more participant said, "I am afraid of road accidents." One participant said, "I am afraid of diseases."

I said, "Chapter 7 has answers to your fears. This chapter has 30 shlokas. I request each participant to read one shloka each that is translated in English." Everyone started reading one after the other.

Knowledge of the Absolute

The Supreme Personality of Godhead said: Now hear, O son of Pritha, how by practicing yoga in full consciousness of Me, with mind attached to Me, you can know Me in full, free from doubt.

I shall now declare unto you in full this knowledge, both exceptionally good and divine. This being known, nothing further shall remain for you to know.

Out of many thousands among men, one may attempt for perfection, and of those who have achieved perfection, hardly one knows Me in truth.

Earth, water, fire, air, ether, mind, intelligence and false ego—all together these eight constitute My separated material energies.

Besides these, O mighty-armed Arjuna, there is another, superior energy of Mine, which comprises the living entities who are exploiting the resources of this material, inferior nature.

All created beings have their source in these two natures. Of all that is material and all that is spiritual in this world, know for certain that I am both the origin and the dissolution.

O conqueror of wealth, there is no truth superior to Me. Everything rests upon Me, as pearls are strung on a thread.

O son of Kunti, I am the taste of water, the light of the sun and the moon, the syllable Om in the Vedic mantras; I am the sound in ether and ability in man.

I am the original fragrance of the earth, and I am the heat in fire. I am the life of all that lives, and I am the penances of all ascetics.

O son of Pritha, know that I am the original seed of all existences, the intelligence of the intelligent, and the courage of all powerful men.

I am the strength of the strong, free of passion and desire. I am sex life that is not contrary to religious principles, O lord of the Bharatas [Arjuna].

Know that all states of being—be they of goodness, passion or ignorance—are manifested by My energy. I am, in one sense, everything, but I am independent. I am not under the modes of material nature, for they, on the contrary, are within me.

Deluded by the three modes [goodness, passion and ignorance], the whole world does not know Me, who am above the modes and infinite.

This divine energy of Mine, consisting of the three modes of material nature, is difficult to overcome. But those who have surrendered unto Me can easily cross beyond it.

Those sinners who are extremely foolish, who are lowest among mankind, whose knowledge is stolen by illusion, and who enter into the atheistic nature of demons, do not surrender unto Me.

O best among the Bharatas, four kinds of religious men begin to render devotional service unto Me—the distressed, the desirer of wealth, the inquisitive, and he who is searching for knowledge of the Absolute.

Of these, the one who is in full knowledge and who is always engaged in pure devotional service is the best. For I am very dear to him, and he is dear to Me.

All these devotees are undoubtedly greathearted souls, but he who is situated in knowledge of Me I consider to be just like My own self. Being engaged in My transcendental service, he is sure to attain Me, the highest and most perfect goal.

After many births and deaths, he who is actually in knowledge surrenders unto Me, knowing Me to be the cause of all causes and all that is. Such a great soul is very rare.

Those whose intelligence has been stolen by material desires surrender unto demigods and follow the particular rules and regulations of worship according to their own natures.

I am in everyone's heart as the Supersoul. As soon as one desires to worship some demigods, I make his faith steady so that he can devote himself to that particular deity.

Blessed with such a faith, he seeks to worship a particular demigod and obtains his desires. But in actuality these benefits are given by Me alone.

Men of small intelligence worship the demigods, and their fruits are limited and temporary. Those who worship the demigods go to the planets of the demigods, but My devotees ultimately reach My supreme planet.

Unintelligent men, who do not know Me perfectly, think that I, the Supreme Personality of Godhead, Krishna, was impersonal before and have now assumed this personality. Due to their small knowledge, they do not know My higher nature, which is imperishable and supreme.

I am never evident to the foolish and unintelligent. For them I am covered by My internal power [maya], and therefore they do not know that I am unborn and flawless.

O Arjuna, as the Supreme Personality of Godhead, I know everything that has happened in the past, all that is happening in the present, and all things that are yet to come. I also know all living entities; but Me no one knows.

O descendant of Bharata, O conqueror of the enemy, all living entities are born into delusion, confused by dualities arisen from desire and hate.

Persons who have acted religiously in previous lives and in this life and whose sinful actions are completely eradicated are freed from the dualities of delusion, and they engage themselves in My service with determination.

Intelligent persons who are trying hard for liberation from old age and death take refuge in Me in devotional service. They are actually Brahman because they entirely know everything about transcendental activities.

Those in full consciousness of Me, who know Me, the Supreme Lord, to be the governing principle of the material manifestation, of the demigods, and of all methods of sacrifice, can understand and know Me, the Supreme Personality of Godhead, even at the time of death.

Now let me Summarize Chapter 7:

Lord Krishna is the Supreme Truth. He is the supreme cause and sustaining force of everything be it material or spiritual. He tells us about his superior (living entities) and inferior (material) energies. Here Lord explains how one can become a fully Krishna conscious person. The beginning of Krishna consciousness is through association of persons who are Krishna conscious. Such association is spiritual and puts one directly in touch with the Supreme Lord, and by His grace, one can understand Krishna to be the Supreme Personality of Godhead. At the same time one can really understand the position of the living entity and how he forgets Krishna and becomes entangled in material activities. By gradual development of Krishna consciousness the living entity understands that due to forgetfulness of Krishna he becomes conditioned by the laws of material nature. He also understands that this human form of life is an opportunity to regain Krishna consciousness to attain causeless mercy of the Supreme Lord.

There are different types of devotees who worship the Supreme Lord: the man in distress, the inquisitive, the man who wants material necessities and wealth, the one seeking knowledge of Paramatma, man seeking liberation from birth, death, old age and diseases. But the one who is in full knowledge of the Lord, who surrenders unto him and engages in devotional service, is very dear to Him. Lord also tells us about the less intelligent men who worship the demigods and how he instills their faith on the demigods and ultimately they reach the planets of the demigods.

I asked everyone, "Can anyone tell me what do you understand from this chapter?" One participant replied, "It talks about how we can become Krishna conscious." The other said, "As we are not aware about Lord's presence we take things in our life for granted." Another participant said, "There are different types of devotees who take shelter of Lord for different reasons." One participant asked, "Madam what about our fears? How can we become fearless?"

I said, "Let me share short stories of different people. I am sure with this all your questions will get answered.

Why Fear, When God Is Here

Pick up the bow with courage, shoot the arrow with faith and kill the target called "Fear". Why Fear, when God is here.

A guy and his girlfriend were returning from a long drive by car on the express highway. The guy was driving at a decent speed, his girlfriend just happen to unlock her seat belt, when suddenly the tyre busted. The guy had good driving skills, because of which he could take the car safely to the side of the highway. But he got scared, as usually at a high speed, when the tyre bursts the car can even tumble or go hay why. His girlfriend sat silently, calm and quite, as if nothing really happened. The guy was trembling and he said, "Are you not afraid? This could have been our last moment of life! Otherwise death was certain. Are you not afraid? Are you mad or something?"

She smiled and said, "Why should I be afraid? I know you drive well and the car is in your hands, why should I be afraid? I know you love me and I also know that God loves me and the situation is in His hands. So whatever is going to happen will be good. If we survive, good; if we don't survive good, because everything is in His hands and He cannot do anything wrong. So why fear, when God is here."

One day some lady asked me, "Are you not afraid of death? Today, we can die any moment. Terrorists have instilled fear within each one of us of death". I smiled and said, "Why fear, when God is here." She asked, "But how can you be so fearless and why doesn't God come and punish those terrorists when they are committing such horrifying crime?" I said, "God is placed in everyone's heart and waiting to kill the demons within them, but unfortunately they have become deaf and blind in killing people. They will be punished in the court of God." The lady asked, "But how can we become fearless, we fear death of ourselves and our loved ones every moment." I said, "Think of God every moment, believe in Him, have faith in Him, take shelter in Him then He will take you away from fear on the boat of fearlessness to a place where you will find peace." She said, "Your words sound good but too flowery, give me a practical answer." I then handed over a book to her and said, "Read one to two pages of this book everyday and you shall experience fearlessness within you." She went home and started reading the book everyday. After 1 year she happened to meet me again. With smiles on her face she said to me, "Thank you, I feel happy and peaceful everyday, I don't know but my fears just vanished from my life." I said, "Don't thank me, it's the power of reading the scared book 'The Bhagavad Gita' on daily basis. Share your secret with others and help them as well." So now, wherever she goes she says, "Why fear, when God is here".

Today I come across many girls and guys who have decided to remain single. They keep telling that many of their relatives push them to get married and settle down. Relatives say, "How can you remain single, life is very difficult to live like that. Are you not afraid to live alone, loneliness will kill you." One of them said, "My grandmother lived alone for many years. My grandfather expired ten years before her. She had three children, one son was married and settled in Germany and both her daughters were married and settled in different cities in India. She lived those ten years in Delhi, all by herself without any help and support. She had strong faith in God and she knew He would take care of her. God did take care of her by giving her many friends in her neighborhood. No wonder she used to always say Why fear, when God is here."

Many years back, I happened to visit my friend's place who had shifted from Delhi to Pune for few years. My visits started happening frequently till the time my friend shifted back to Delhi and we lost touch. Today after many years we shared memories of our good old friendship. Recently I happened to learn a shocking thing, the rented house my friend was staying in was haunted. "Oh my God! You idiot why didn't you tell me at that time, I would have certainly fled out of fear. But how come you managed to stay with them for few years, you could have easily shifted to another apartment", I said in despair. My friend said, "Even I was sacred when I came to know about ghosts in my house. But after sometime I realized they were friendly ghosts and played pranks to shoo off all my friends and family. I guess they liked you too." I was surprised and shocked, "Hey listen I don't like all these ghosts stories, please tell me you are lying." My friend said, "I am not lying. It is 100% true, you can ask neighbors staying there. The one thing that kept me strong was my prayer to God and I realized that they do not trouble pious souls. I suppose that's why you didn't come to know of their presence around you." After hearing this story, I realized it was my reading of The Bhagavad Gita that protected me from them. Such are the powers of reading The Bhagavad Gita, so Why fear, when God is here.

Lord Krishna guided Arjuna on the battlefield of Kurukshetra and told him not to be afraid of killing his own blood relatives because you are fighting this war for Dharma. Lord Krishna said, "Kill that fear within you, rise up and fight." Human beings when faced with crimes, accidents, diseases and deaths in worst circumstances than realize their association with God and start praying asking for help. Lord Krishna said, "Don't forget Me else you will remain entangled in your miseries. Think of Me always, worship Me and you will attain causeless mercy from Me." Don't be afraid of accidents, death, bomb blasts, old age, loneliness, ghosts, diseases and threats; just kill the target called fear, by shooting the arrow with faith. Why fear, when God is here. With this comes a very important life lesson.

**Lesson No: 15 Don't be afraid of death, old age, diseases and threats. Kill this fear, by shooting the arrow with faith. Have faith in God that He will protect you. Read the Bhagavad Gita daily, it will help you become fearless. Why fear, when God is here.

Shikha raised her hand, "Yes Shikha any questions?" She said, "As a woman I am scared of something called as Rape. I am sure many parents are scared and concerned every now and then of their daughters safety. How can we as women become fearless in this?"

I said, "Shikha you have touched a very sensitive issue, faced by many girls and women. To answer this let me share something with all of you on this. Some may agree but again it boils down to faith.

Have Faith In God

One day a big seminar was organized by Girls College, inviting all the girls and their parents from other colleges, to discuss and find solutions about the most fearful topic "Rape". Now Lord Krishna came to know about it and He too thought of attending. So He some how self invited Himself and become a keynote speaker in the discussion panel. This time He disguised Himself as a consultant.

As the discussion panel entered into the question and answer session where everyone was talking, Lord Krishna was just listening. Parents were fuming at the insecurity they feel when their teenage daughter goes out. Parents started shouting, "We want safety and security of our children." Lord Krishna then took the mike and said, "Do you have faith in God?" The Parents got puzzled as to what kind of a question is that, is it even relevant? He then went to the dice and spoke, "When you don't have faith in God, how can you expect your child to be safe?" Then one parent said, "What can God do about it, He is just sitting somewhere and quietly seeing this crime happening and not even doing anything about it." Lord Krishna said, "So what do you expect God to do, send some Superman to rescue all girls and women right at the darkest hour, at that very moment to save your child." Everyone was quite.

Lord Krishna further said, "Do you know what happened in the Mahabharata? When the Kauravas tried to disrobed Draupadi by removing her sari in hall full of people, she requested her five husbands to rescue her from this evil but they stood there helplessly, then she asked all the elders present in the hall for help but they too remained silent, then finally she prayed to Lord Krishna for help. He immediately protected Draupadi from the shame of being disrobed by making her cloth become endless. The Lord took care of her honor and punished the sinners during the battle of Mahabharata. One parent enquired, "But how is it relevant today?" Lord Krishna said, "The fact that Lord protected Draupadi when she was being disrobed itself says that God helps when prayed or called for at the moment of darkness.

When any girl is dragged into this horrifying event, God does warn her, her parents and her loved ones of something evil that might happen. But we tend to ignore and do not understand these warnings. God does His best to speak loud from within, like 'don't go or stop' but we ignore."

Then one parent said, "What you are saying is going above my head, do you have a short cut solution to this?" Lord Krishna smiled and said, "Just pray, ask God to help and He will help." One girl after listening to all this conversation asked, "How can a girl think of God at that moment, she is already so scared and frightened?" Lord Krishna said, "That's a very good question. You need to practice thinking of God every moment, not just when you want something you think of God. Become conscious or aware of God within yourself that means become 'Krishna Consciousness'. Have faith in God." Another girl stood up and asked, "How can the girl child below 12 years be saved from his horrifying crime?" Lord Krishna said,

"The men who commit such crime are definitely punished by God, of this there is no doubt. Children must also do the same thing pray to God at that moment. Parents need to be alert and aware of their children whereabouts and pay attention to their day-to-day activities. God certainly helps but only thing you need to remember is to have faith and pray to Him in the darkest hour."

Lord Krishna said, "Let me share with you a story of faith in this context."

"One dark evening, a young working professional girl was on her way home after attending dinner party at her office. She got into a cab that was to take her home.

Minutes later she found that her mobile had discharged completely and she started to feel uncomfortable. The driver realized it and took advantage of this situation to turn the car onto a darker road. The girl felt something is wrong. The girl also realized that the driver was not the one with the same identity as mentioned in the cab, he seemed to have replaced the original one for few rides. She immediately told the cab driver to stop but he didn't listen and drove even faster. The driver took the cab to the darkest corner of a street with no traffic and streetlights not working. The girl got very scared and she thought to jump out of the cab only to realize that the cab is internally locked. Even if she cried for help no one would hear.

The cab stopped and the driver was about to make his move to molest her. She immediately took a deep breath believed in herself and at that very moment she decided to pray to God and asked for her safety. She kept on praying asking for help. The cab driver laughed thinking there is no way anyone will come to save her from me. Immediately police cab came from nowhere to check why has a commercial cab stopped in a dark place. The girl rushed out to tell her horrifying story and the cab driver was arrested.

The girl thanked the police and asked, "How is it that you came to know I am in trouble and came at the right time to help me?" The police told her that we are continuously doing surveillance from our control room and anything we see and feel is not right we immediately send our team to check.

We need nothing to worry about. For God is always there by our side to help us. All we need to do is to call His name and ask for help. And also have faith in God."

The entire audience stood up and clapped for such an enlightening speech and went home with a sign of contentment.

In the Bhagavad Gita, Lord Krishna also told Arjuna to become fully Krishna conscious and that this human form of life is an opportunity to regain Krishna consciousness to attain causeless mercy of the Supreme Lord. When one is fully Krishna conscious, means being aware of Krishna within himself or herself he or she never gets entangled in material activities nor gets conditioned by material nature. He gains full knowledge of Krishna, surrenders unto Krishna and engages in devotional service of Krishna. Here comes another life lesson.

**Lesson No: 16 Have faith in God. Pray to Him and ask for help in your darkest moment. Always be alert and aware of what God tries to tell us. Have faith in the Divine within you.

Now it's time for a short tea break. Time is 4 pm and we all will gather again at 4.20 pm.

CHAPTER 8

Remember Me Always

"Welcome back from this short and sweet tea break. Hope you all are feeling refreshed. We are now going to play a game. I want you all to think of one person who is very close to you could be your husband, wife, boyfriend, girlfriend, your child, your parent, your best friend or just about anyone. Irrespective of what your current status with that person is, be it good, bad, sour doesn't matter. I want you all to write down all the things you appreciate about that person. Think of all the good things good memories you had in the past with that person, write it down. Any incident that makes you laugh or smile, write it down. Time is 3 minutes."

"Now I want you all to choose your favorite corner of this room. Call that person now and say Thank you for all the things you wrote down. Don't worry of what that person will think, is it right time or not. Just call and appreciate that person for being there in your life. Time is 3 minutes." Everyone got busy calling his or her special someone. Few participants even got very emotional when talking. After time was up, everyone got back to their respective seats. "How was the experience?" I asked. One said, "I had never said Thank you to my dad, it was just an amazing feeling." Another said, "First time after so many months me and my husband smiled and laughed." Shikha said, "As relationship turns sour over a period of time, we tend to forget all the good qualities of that person and by thanking we feel even more good than the one receiving it." I said, "Great. Amazing experience isn't it? That's the power of Gratitude and how it is related to Chapter 8 of The Bhagavad Gita we will find out.

This chapter has 28 shlokas. I request each participant to read one shloka each that is translated in English." Everyone started reading one after the other.

Attaining the Supreme

Arjuna inquired: O my Lord, O Supreme Person, what is Brahman? What is the self? What are fruitive activities? What is this material manifestation? And what are the demigods? Please explain this to me.

Who is the Lord of sacrifice, and how does He live in the body, O Madhusudana? And how can those engaged in devotional service know You at the time of death?

The Supreme Personality of Godhead said: The indestructible, transcendental living entity is called Brahman, and his everlasting nature is called adhyatma, the self. Action pertaining to the development of the material bodies of the living entities is called karma, or fruitive activities.

O best of the embodied beings, the physical nature, which is constantly changing, is called adhibhuta [the material manifestation]. The universal form of the Supreme Lord, which includes all the demigods, like those of the sun and moon, is called adhideva. And I, the Supreme Lord, represented as the Supersoul in the heart of every embodied being, am called adhiyajna [the Lord of sacrifice].

And whoever, at the end of his life, quits his body remembering Me alone at once attains My nature. Of this there is no doubt.

Whatever state of being one remembers when he quits his body, O son of Kunti, that state he will attain without fail.

Therefore, Arjuna, you should always think of Me in the form of Krishna and at the same time carry out your prescribed duty of fighting. With your activities dedicated to Me and your mind and intelligence fixed on Me, you will attain Me without doubt.

He who meditates on Me as the Supreme Personality of Godhead, his mind constantly engaged in remembering Me, undeviated from the path, he, O Partha is sure to reach Me.

One should meditate upon the Supreme Person as the one who knows everything, as He who is the oldest, who is the controller, who is smaller than the smallest, who is the maintainer of everything, who is beyond all material conception, who is unimaginable, and who is always a person. He is luminous like the sun, and He is transcendental, beyond this material nature.

One who, at the time of death, fixes his life air between the eyebrows and, by the strength of yoga, with an undeviating mind, engages himself in remembering the Supreme Lord in full devotion, will certainly attain to the Supreme Personality of Godhead.

Persons who are learned in the Vedas, who utter omkara and who are great sages in the renounced order enter into Brahman. Desiring such perfection, one practices celibacy. I shall now briefly explain to you this process by which one may attain freedom from the effects of sins.

The yogic situation is that of detachment from all sensual engagements. Closing all the doors of the senses and fixing the mind on the heart and the life air at the top of the head, one establishes himself in yoga.

After being situated in this yoga practice and vibrating the sacred syllable om, the supreme combination of letters, if one thinks of the Supreme Personality of Godhead and quits his body, he will certainly reach the spiritual planets.

For one who always remembers Me without deviation, I am easy to obtain, O son of Pritha, because of his constant engagement in devotional service.

After attaining Me, the great souls, who are yogis in devotion, never return to this temporary world, which is full of miseries, because they have attained the highest perfection.

From the highest planet in the material world down to the lowest, all are places of misery wherein repeated birth and death take place. But one who attains to My abode, O son of Kunti, never takes birth again.

By human calculation, a thousand ages taken together form the duration of Brahma's one day. And such also is the duration of his night.

At the beginning of Brahma's day, all living entities become manifest from the unmanifest state, and thereafter, when the night falls, they are merged into the unmanifest again.

Again and again, when Brahma's day arrives, all living entities come into being, and with the arrival of Brahma's night they are helplessly destroyed.

Yet there is another unmanifest nature, which is eternal and is transcendental to this manifested and unmanifested matter. It is supreme and is never destroyed. When all in this world is destroyed, that part remains as it is.

That which the Vedantists describe as unmanifest and flawless, that which is known as the supreme destination, that place from which, having attained it, one never returns---that is My supreme home.

The Supreme Personality of Godhead, who is greater than all, is attainable by pure devotion. Although He is present in His home, He is present everywhere, and everything is situated within Him.

O best of the Bharatas, I shall now explain to you the different times at which, passing away from this world, the yogi does or does not come back.

Those who know the Supreme Brahman attain that Supreme by passing away from the world during the influence of the fiery god, in the light, at an auspicious moment of the day, during the fortnight of the waxing moon, or during the six months when the sun travels in the north.

The mystic who passes away from this world during the smoke, the night, the fortnight of the waning moon, or the six months when the sun passes to the south reaches the moon planet but again comes back.

According to Vedic opinion, there are two ways of passing from this world—one in light and one in darkness. When one passes in light, he does not come back; but when one passes in darkness, he returns.

Although the devotees know these two paths, O Arjuna, they are never confused. Therefore be always fixed in devotion.

A person who accepts the path of devotional service is not deprived of the results derived from studying the Vedas, performing severe sacrifices, giving charity or pursuing philosophical and fruitive activities. Simply by performing devotional service, he attains all these, and at the end he reaches the supreme eternal abode.

Now let me Summarize Chapter 8:

When a devotee remembers Lord Krishna throughout his or her life, especially at the time of death, one reaches His supreme abode, which is beyond this material world. Lord confirms that once you attain Him there is no return to this temporary world full of miseries, because you have attained the highest perfection. The easiest way of God realization is to always remember God and do your duty.

I asked everyone, "Can anyone tell me what do you understand from this chapter?" One participant replied, "We must always remember God." The other said, "If someone remembers Lord at the time of death, then there is no coming back to this temporary world of misery." One participant asked, "Madam what's the connection of gratitude and remembering Lord?"

I said, "Good question and the answer to it is.

Gratitude is the way to Bliss

Have you ever gone to a temple and thanked God for whatever He has given you? Sadly, the answer I mostly hear is "No, we always go to ask Him for something or the other." It's been many years, whenever I go to a temple or any holy place; I just thank God for everything He has given me. Try it, you will feel happy and blessed.

Thanking God for the desires or wishes you want fulfilled when the chance of getting it is hardly there, is indeed a very difficult process. For desires to manifest or wishes to fulfill, we need to have full faith in God. A friend of mine was having issues with her boyfriend. They used to often have fights, arguments and innumerable breakups and patch ups. I suggested her to write down all the things she appreciates and likes about her boyfriend. Be grateful to have that person in your life everyday. Slowly as days passed, their fights came down and they eventually started caring and loving each other because she started to focus on the good things positive side about her boyfriend and ignored the negatives. Now, she thanks God for giving her such a loving, caring and understanding boyfriend. Gratitude is the way to a blissful relationship.

My grandmother used to thank each person for every small little thing they helped her with. She also made a beautiful practice of thanking God after every small little work that got completed. Before eating, she used to thank God for giving her good food and good health. This way I too started practicing gratitude everyday. This has bought immense peacefulness within me. Now, I thank God for each and every thing. Gratitude is the way to a blissful life.

In the Bhagavad Gita, Lord Krishna tells Arjuna that anyone who at the time of death, remembers Me, surely comes to My supreme home and never returns to this temporary world which is full of miseries. Gratitude is one of the easiest ways to remember God always. Gratitude is the way to a blissful afterlife.

Gratitude has become my daily thanks giving prayer to God. After I get ready, I start my day by reading 2 Shlokas of the Bhagavad Gita then I thank God for giving me good healthy body, a calm positive and focused mind, a beautiful house, happy family, awesome friends and peaceful relationship, lots of love and care, help me with the right investments and help me write this wonderful book. Try thanking God whenever you go to temple, thank God for fulfilling your desires and wishes giving you peaceful relationships. Thank God always by remembering Him, thank God for each and every thing He has given you and in return you will experience bliss. Everyone make a note of this simple yet impactful life lesson.

**Lesson No: 17 Thank God whenever you pray to Him at home or when you go to temple. Thank God for each and every thing He has given you. Thank God for fulfilling all your wishes and giving you peaceful relationships. Gratitude is the easiest way to remember God.

I said, "By Thanking God every time is indeed the simplest way to remember Him always in today's life." One participant raised his hand and asked, "I totally agree that we remember God only when we are in trouble or when we have a problem or when we need something. Is there any other way to remember God other than gratitude?"

I smiled and said, "Hear this interesting conversation between Lord Krishna and Arjuna."

Do My Work

One day Arjuna was sitting with Lord Krishna in a garden under a tree. A question came to Arjuna's mind and he thought of asking it to Lord Krishna, "My dearest friend I have a question in mind, would like to ask You?" Lord Krishna said, "Go ahead, I'm listening." Arjuna said, "21st century is going on, the world is changing very fast. Technology has transformed everyone's life and human beings are busy making money for themselves. Everyone is busy, nobody is bothered about anyone. But still they are suffering in this world. They are not happy. Why?

Lord Krishna said, "Good question my friend. Human beings face two kinds of sufferings, one physical and other mental. Physical sufferings that they face is because of their past karmas or deeds. Mental suffering is because of their forgetfulness of Me. People only remember Me when they are facing a grave problem, otherwise I don't even come on their minds."

Arjuna asked, "So what can we do about this? How can people remember You?

Lord Krishna said, "People pray to Me only when they have a problem. But very few are genuinely interested to know Me, few take interest in finding more about Me, few become My devotee. For them I'm always there on their minds and in their hearts guiding them because they truly believe in Me, love Me and listen to Me. I cannot force anyone to think about Me all the time or pray to Me. The need has to come from within to know Me and love Me, not just to remember Me when they are in pain."

"People can remember Me in three ways:

First while remembering Me, they do their duties.

Second while doing their duties, they remember Me.

Third they only do My work."

Most of the people try to follow first and second way, but they struggle to remember Me and they forget. People get busy with their work, family, relationships and business because of which I am forgotten again and again and it becomes difficult for them to remember Me. If one only does My work, then I will always be remembered. So one should only do My work so that one can always remember Me."

Arjuna enquired, "Lord can You explain what is Your work?"

Lord Krishna said, "To do My work, one must accept and understand the truth that everything belongs to Me. All human beings and living entities are part of Me and I am present in everyone. Actually everyone does My work but the problem is that people think that they are working for themselves. As soon as one gives up this thought that whatever he is doing is for himself and accepts the truth that everything belongs to Me. All work becomes My work. One should accept this that I'm the proprietor of everything your house, business, work. With My blessings, one must think that he is only doing My work for the happiness and pleasure of people around who are Mine. Then there will be no effort required in remembering Me."

In the Bhagavad Gita, Lord Krishna told Arjuna that, "You should always think of Me and at the same time carry out your duties as Kshatriya. You should dedicate all your activities to Me and fix your mind and intelligence on Me. Your mind must be constantly engaged in remembering Me, undeviating from this path, you will reach Me." Here comes another life lesson.

Lesson No: 18 Remember God always. Work for God. Think of God anytime and everywhere. Pray to Him when you are in trouble.

CHAPTER 9

Arjuna Engage In Devotional Service

"Let me ask all of you a question, what comes to your mind when the word 'God' comes?" Someone said, "Bhajan, kirtan (religious songs)". Another person said, "Praying in front of deity in temples". One said, "Attending satsungs (religious gatherings), listening to religious songs and stories of Lord." I said, "Great. Would you all like to hear a bhajan inspired from a Bollywood movie song?" Everyone nodded. Interestingly the song was so famous common and melodious that everyone started singing together and enjoyed the process that they had never experienced before.

"Chapter 9 is about devotional service. This chapter has 34 shlokas. I request each participant to read one shloka each that is translated in English." Everyone started reading one after the other.

The Most Confidential Knowledge

The Supreme Personality of Godhead said: My dear Arjuna, because you are never envious of Me, I shall impart to you this most confidential knowledge and realization, knowing which you shall be relieved of the miseries of material existence.

This knowledge is the king of education, the most secret of all secrets. It is the purest knowledge, and because it gives direct awareness of the self by realization, it is the perfection of religion. It is everlasting, and it is joyfully performed.

Those who are not faithful in this devotional service cannot attain Me, O conqueror of enemies. Therefore they return to the path of birth and death in this material world.

By Me, in My unmanifested form, this entire universe is present. All beings are in Me, but I am not in them.

And yet everything that is created does not rest in Me. Witness My spiritual splendor! Although I am the maintainer of all living entities and although I am everywhere, I am not a part of this cosmic manifestation, for My Self is the very source of creation.

Understand that as the mighty wind, blowing everywhere, rests always in the sky, all created beings rest in Me.

O son of Kunti, at the end of the millennium all material manifestations enter into My nature, and at the beginning of another millennium, by My power, I create them again.

The whole cosmic order is under Me. Under My will it is automatically appearing again and again, and under My will it is destroyed at the end.

O Dhananjaya, all this work cannot bind Me. I am ever detached from all these material activities, seated as though neutral.

This material nature, which is one of My energies, is working under My direction, O son of Kunti, producing all moving and non-moving beings. Under its rule this manifestation is created and destroyed again and again.

Fools laugh at Me when I descend in the human form. They do not know My transcendental nature as the Supreme Lord of all that be.

Those who are thus confused are attracted by evil and don't believe in existence of God. In that misleading condition, their hopes for freedom, their fruitive activities, and their culture of knowledge are all defeated.

O son of Pritha, those who are not mislead, the great souls, are under the protection of the divine nature. They are fully engaged in devotional service because they know Me as the Supreme Personality of Godhead, original and infinite.

Always chanting My glories, making an effort with great determination, bowing down before Me, these great souls constantly worship Me with devotion.

Others, who engage in sacrifice by the cultivation of knowledge, worship the Supreme Lord as the one without a second, as diverse in many, and in the universal form.

But it is I who am the ritual, I the sacrifice, the offering to the ancestors, the healing herb, the transcendental chant. I am the butter and the fire and the offering.

I am the father of this universe, the mother, the support and the grandfather. I am the object of knowledge, the purifier and the syllable om. I am also the Rig, the Sama and the Yajur Vedas.

I am the goal, the maintainer, the master, the witness, the home, the refuge and the most dear friend. I am the creation and the destruction, the basis of everything, the resting place and the everlasting seed.

O Arjuna, I give heat, and I withhold and send forth the rain. I am immortality, and I am also death personified. Both soul and physical being are in Me.

Those who study the Vedas and drink the soma juice, seeking the heavenly planets, worship Me indirectly. Purified of sinful reactions, they take birth on the religious, heavenly planet of Indra, where they enjoy godly delights.

When they have thus enjoyed vast heavenly sense pleasure and the results of their religious activities are exhausted, they return to this mortal planet again. Thus those who seek sense enjoyment by adhering to the principles of the three Vedas achieve only repeated birth and death.

But those who always worship Me with exclusive devotion, meditating on My transcendental form-to them I carry what they lack, and I preserve what they have.

Those who are devotees of other gods and who worship them with faith actually worship only Me, O son of Kunti, but they do so in a wrong way.

I am the only enjoyer and master of all sacrifices. Therefore, those who do not recognize My true transcendental nature fall down.

Those who worship the demigods will take birth among the demigods; those who worship the ancestors go to the ancestors; those who worship ghosts and spirits will take birth among such beings; and those who worship Me will live with Me.

If one offers Me with love and devotion a leaf, a flower, a fruit or water, I will accept it.

Whatever you do, whatever you eat, whatever you offer or give away, and whatever strict actions you perform—do that, O son of Kunti, as an offering to Me.

In this way you will be freed from bondage to work and its auspicious and inauspicious results. With your mind fixed on Me in this principle of renunciation you will become free and come to Me.

I envy no one, nor am I partial to anyone. I am equal to all. But whoever gives service unto Me in devotion is a friend, is in Me, and I am also a friend to him.

Even if one commits the most terrible action, if he is engaged in devotional service, he is to be considered saintly because he is properly situated in his determination.

He quickly becomes worthy and attains lasting peace. O son of Kunti, declare it boldly that My devotee never perishes.

O son of Pritha, those who take shelter in Me, though they be of lower birth--women, vaishyas [merchants], as well as shudras [workers]-- can attain the supreme destination.

How much more this is so of the worthy brahmanas, the devotees and the saintly kings. Therefore, having come to this temporary, miserable world, engage in loving service unto Me.

Engage your mind always in thinking of Me, become My devotee, offer respect to Me and worship Me. Being completely absorbed in Me, surely you will come to Me.

Now Let Me Summarize Chapter 9:

Lord Krishna tells Arjuna about the most confidential knowledge knowing which he will be relieved from the miseries of this materialistic world. Lord Krishna is the Supreme God and the Supreme object of worship. The great souls know Krishna by engaging in transcendental devotional service (bhakti), come under the protection of His divine nature. By always thinking of Krishna, becoming his pure devotee, by worshipping Him, one returns to Krishna.

Lord Krishna loves everyone equally, but He takes personal interest in His devotees and becomes their friend. His devotees become worthy and attain lasting peace. Anyone who takes shelter in Lord Krishna can reach his Supreme destination.

I asked everyone, "Can anyone tell me what do you understand from this chapter?" One participant replied, "We must engage in devotional service of God." The other said, "Lord Krishna is the Supreme God and Supreme object of worship." One participant asked, "When we become devotee Lord takes special care of us." Another participant said, "Madam today so many people are dying of cancer, why doesn't Lord protect us and save us?" I said, "Good question and the answer is.

Divine Food Healthy Food

What is Divine food? In the Bhagavad Gita, Lord Krishna mentioned that if someone offers Him with love and devotion a leaf, a flower, a fruit or water, He will accept it. Whatever you do, whatever you eat, whatever you offer or give away, and whatever strict actions you perform do that as an offering to Lord Krishna. The food you offer to God becomes prasadam 'Divine food'.

What is Healthy food? When you eat prasadam all negativity in the food is destroyed and it becomes positive and healthy. If a devotee starts eating food offered to God first, he surely would live a healthy and positive life.

One morning a group of middle-aged men and women who regularly meet at a park and have their daily walks were sitting and having a chat. One man said, "Do you know my neighbor recently got diagnosed with Cancer. He is in 3rd stage of his illness fighting each day like a warrior." One lady said, "Oh he is such a humble man, what a loving family and see what is happening." Another man said, "Now a days we hear many cases of people suffering from Cancer and many other diseases." Third man in the group said, "We take care of our well being so much, eat healthy, do our daily walks, do exercise, do yoga, but still there is no guarantee that we will be able to protect ourselves, our family and friends from it."

A priest who comes everyday to pick flowers in the park happened to hear these conversations. One lady within the group looked at him and spoke loudly, "Even God keeps quite and just sees good people suffering from various diseases on earth and does nothing to help and protect them." The priest said, "God has provided us with abundance of food in form of fruits, vegetables, water, food grains and much more. What are the people doing to it? Adding chemicals and fertilizers beyond a limit to make them grow faster in order to sell it at a better price. Everything we eat today is adulterated at the cost of everyone's health. People now have come to this realization and moved to healthy eating."

The priest who was a doctor earlier further said, "Let me explain you the basic concept of our body, any form of disease strives and grows in an acidic environment. We need the right food to help neutralize our body to alkaline environment and maintain the right pH balance in our body. This can be achieved by having a balanced diet in our meal."

The priest said, "There is another way to bring positivity into your daily meals. When the lady of the house is cooking food for the entire family, on the music system, which plays divine songs (bhajans) or chants name of your Lord. This will start adding positive vibrations into your food that will help you remain healthy and positive all day. Even in today's fast paced lifestyle we are so used to eating food from outside, before eating just chant the Lord's name and have a good meal."

"You need not fear from the negativity that has entered in your food, just offer it to Lord Krishna and He will transform it into positive, healthy and happy food." Everyone looked at the priest and applauded after hearing these great insights.

Once a wife wanted to divorce her husband due to aggressive and abusive behavior. The problem was not with the husband but with the unhealthy lifestyle and eating habits. Today we are eating junk food, unhealthy food. Not having proper meals, skipping meals. Eating meals while driving or while working on desk or while on mobile phones or when watching TV. Can we not devote just 10min to eat healthy meals at peace? By skipping meals or eating unhealthy food the acidic levels in our body increases, which is directly responsible for the aggressive and abusive behavior. If you don't eat healthy food happy food at proper intervals, you start feeling restless and angry. Taking care of what and when you eat will lead you to a better life and better relationships. This teaches us another life lesson.

Lesson No: 19 Eat food offered to God first that's prasadam 'Divine food' to stay happy and healthy. While cooking or before you eat food just chant Lord Krishna's name to remove negativity in the food.

One participant raised his hand and asked, "Are there some more practical benefits of chanting and listening to devotional songs?" Another participant asked, "Why was The Bhagavad Gita told to only Arjuna by Lord Krishna?" I said, "Listen to this interesting story.

Krishna, Krishna, Krishna

Death is a reality a bitter truth that can happen to anyone at any time and at any age. A middle-aged woman recently went through a trauma of loosing her beloved husband and only child in a car accident. Her beautiful and only family disappeared in thin air never to come back. She didn't have any relatives or friends and felt lonely day by day. She cursed herself cried from within as to why didn't she die with them, why did God save her and took them away? Why?

Lord Krishna knew this lady was in pain and He wanted to help her. So He decided to disguise as a middle-aged woman and became the neighbor of this depressed and lonely lady. Now Lord Krishna in the disguise of a woman sang amazing divine songs to create a positive change in the heart of this lady. Lord made it a point to blow conch shell every morning to release positive vibrations and drive away negativity. Soon the lady wanted to meet her neighbor and appreciate the great divine songs she sings which helps her in relaxing. The depressed and lonely lady finally goes and meets her neighbor and says, "I really like the divine songs you sing everyday it creates a positive effect within me. Who are you? What do you do?"

Lord Krishna said, "I am your friend and your neighbor. I sing divine songs and chant Lord's name to heal the souls around. I am aware of what you have gone through. Like you we all have lost someone dear but we must not let negativity against the divine take place within us. It's indeed a very difficult phase to deal with but we must accept and respect the decision of the divine instead of cursing the Lord. Our entire life revolves around our family but when we are left alone only God becomes our best friend and family, when we fall in love and devote ourselves completely to the divine we begin to feel at peace."

The depressed and lonely lady asked Lord Krishna, "How can listening to divine songs and chanting Lord's name help us?"

Lord Krishna said, "Do you know that chanting mantras and listening to divine songs (bhajans) have amazing benefits on our mind, heart, body and soul? It helps remove negativity, reduces stress, anxiety and worrying issues. It helps improve blood circulation, controls blood pressure, removes toxins and helps to stay focused and improve concentration. It also helps regularize our sleep pattern."

"Many a times we are overcome by negative thoughts or negative emotions or negative vibrations like anger, sadness, disappointment, depression and so on. Just by chanting, the vibrations within our body changes that immediately drive away negativity and help us understand and identify the positive things. By chanting and repetition of mantras, you begin to get positive thoughts, divine thoughts and positive energy flows into your mind. When the mind is purified all the 5 enemies of the mind-lust, anger, attachment, greed, ego runs away."

"Chanting not only of mantras has a positive effect but chanting and repeating positive words and affirmations has a similar effect. Whenever you feel negative just start chanting or repeating positive words like a mantra of your life for example 'I am feeling peaceful within myself' or 'I love my life'. Remember Aamir Khan's mantra 'All is well' in his movie 3 Idiots. In modern age we are not used to chanting Lord name and singing divine songs, if you can do so it will be a great boon for you else chanting and repeating positive words and affirmations will keep you going in the long run."

Lord Krishna said, "Let Me share an interesting story mentioned in Bhagavatam Katha of Lord Krishna and Arjuna. This will answer why Arjuna is Lord Krishna's favorite devotee and what is the benefit of chanting.

Once upon a time Krishna and Arjuna were returning to Dwarka. Arjuna was handling the chariot, so when they reached Dwarka he was tired and went to the guesthouse to sleep. Dwarka was Lord Krishna's home at that time. After a while, Rukmini came to Lord Krishna and announced that food was ready. Rukmini was Lord Krishna's first wife. Lord Krishna said that we have a guest at home and I will not eat till he is ready. So Rukmini went to wake up Arjuna. When she got to his room, she was so surprised to see that each and every part, each and every pore of his body was chanting "Krishna Krishna Krishna" even as he was sleeping!!! Seeing this amazing sight, she got transfixed and started clapping her hands. Narada Muni showed up and told Lord Krishna your food is getting cold; and then he went to wake up Arjuna. Narada Muni is the divine messenger of Lord Vishnu. When he saw the same sight, he too got transfixed and started playing his veena. Satyabhama then came to call the Lord to eat, and then she said she will go wake up Arjuna. Satyabhama was Lord Krishna's second wife. When she got to his room and saw him chanting in his sleep, Rukmini clapping and Narada Muni playing the veena, she forgot about the food and started dancing.

Finally, Lord Krishna decided to go and wake up Arjuna Himself. When He reached there and saw all of them, His heart started overflowing with love and He sat on the bed and started massaging the feet of Arjuna. Arjuna woke up with a start and said Lord what are you doing?

The Lord said, you love me with each and every pore of your body, and this is why you are so dear to me! Saying this, He warmly embraced Arjuna!

Lord Krishna looked at everyone and said now you know why Arjuna is my favorite. He loves Me so much that he is calling My name even in his sleep. This is how anyone can become My pure devotee just by chanting My name."

Lord Krishna disguised as neighbor said to the depressed lady, "I hope you have found the answers to your whys." The depressed lady smiled after a long time and thanked her neighbor for the much needed help.

In the Bhagavad Gita, Lord Krishna mentioned to Arjuna on the battlefield of Kurukshetra the most confidential knowledge that He is indeed the Supreme Personality of Godhead, Original and everlasting. Great souls are under His protection, they know Him and engage themselves in His devotional service. There are fools who laugh at Him when He descends in human form because they don't know His spiritual nature. His devotees always chant His glories, bow down before Him, respect Him and constantly worship Him with devotion. This teaches us another important life lesson.

Lesson No: 20 Worship God in full devotion by chanting His name "Krishna, Krishna, Krishna." Chanting Lord Krishna's name and listening to divine songs drives away feelings of loneliness, stress, anxiety, depression and negativity.

It's 5.30 pm and we have come to the end of Day 1 Spiritual session. You all are free to spend rest of the evening all by yourself or join us at 7pm at the reception; the tour bus will take us to Panjim, Goa. Tomorrow we will all assemble at 7 am at the beach same place for yoga session followed by meditation. I will meet you all at this very seminar hall at 10am after breakfast."

CHAPTER 10

I Am Within You

"Good morning everyone. How are you all doing? Hope you all had lovely breakfast and also enjoyed the yoga and meditation session." One participant said, "Madam, many didn't even get up." I said, "No worries. Let's quickly do a recap of what we learnt yesterday. Chapter 1 we learnt about thinking positive and accepting good and bad in any relationship. Chapter 2 we learnt about the importance of having a best friend and psychological representations of all characters in the picture of The Bhagavad Gita. Chapter 3 we learnt about doing our duty and finding our passion by analyzing our strengths and weaknesses. Chapter 4 we learnt about intuition and how to surrender to Lord Krishna. Chapter 5 we learnt how to see God in everyone, understand vibrations and hear our inner voice, also about the need to help others. Chapter 6 we learnt about meditation, de-addict our habits, how to meditate and connect with the Supersoul within ourselves. Chapter 7 we learnt how to overcome fears and have faith in Lord Krishna. Chapter 8 we learnt about importance of gratitude and how we can always remember God by doing work for God. Chapter 9 we learnt the importance of having divine food healthy food and chanting mantras.

It's time to begin with chapter 10. This chapter has 42 shlokas. I request each participant to read one shloka each that is translated in English." Everyone started reading one after the other.

The Opulence of the Absolute

The Supreme Personality of Godhead said: Listen again, O mighty-armed Arjuna. Because you are My dear friend, for your benefit I shall speak to you further, giving knowledge that is better than what I have already explained.

Neither the hosts of demigods nor the great sages know My origin or opulence, for, in every respect, I am the source of the demigods and sages.

He who knows Me as the unborn, as the beginningless, as the Supreme Lord of all the worlds—he only, undeluded among men, is freed from all sins.

Intelligence, knowledge, freedom from doubt and delusion, forgiveness, truthfulness, control of the senses, control of the mind, happiness and sorrow, birth, death, fear, fearlessness, nonviolence, calmness, satisfaction, severity, charity, fame and disgrace--all these various qualities of living beings are created by Me alone.

The seven great sages and before them the four other great sages and the Manus [originator of mankind] come from Me, born from My mind, and all the living beings populating the various planets descend from them.

One who is factually convinced of this opulence and spiritual power of Mine engages in pure devotional service; of this there is no doubt.

I am the source of all spiritual and material worlds. Everything originates from Me. The wise who perfectly know this engage in My devotional service and worship Me with all their hearts.

The thoughts of My pure devotees dwell in Me, their lives are fully devoted to My service, and they derive great satisfaction and bliss from always enlightening one another and conversing about Me.

To those who are constantly devoted to serving Me with love, I give the understanding by which they can come to Me.

To show them special mercy, I, dwelling in their hearts, destroy with the shining lamp of knowledge the darkness born of ignorance.

Arjuna said: You are the Supreme Personality of Godhead, the ultimate home, the purest, the Absolute Truth. You are the everlasting, transcendental, original person, the unborn, the greatest. All the great sages such as Narada, Asita, Devala and Vyasa confirm this truth about You, and now You Yourself are declaring it to me.

O Krishna, I totally accept as truth all that You have told me. Neither the demigods nor the demons, O Lord, can understand Your personality.

Indeed, You alone know Yourself by Your own internal power, O Supreme Person, origin of all, Lord of all beings, God of gods, Lord of the universe!

Please tell me in detail of Your divine opulence by which You are present in all these worlds.

O Krishna, O supreme mystic, how shall I constantly think of You, and how shall I know You? In what various forms are You to be remembered, O Supreme Personality of Godhead?

O Janardana [Krishna], again please describe in detail the mystic power of Your opulence, I am never satisfied in hearing about You, for the more I hear the more I want to taste the nectar of Your words.

The Supreme Personality of Godhead said: Yes, I will tell you of My splendorous manifestations, but only of those which are important, O Arjuna, for My opulence is limitless.

I am the Supersoul, O Arjuna, seated in the hearts of all living entities. I am the beginning, the middle and the end of all beings.

Of the Adityas I am Vishnu, of lights I am the radiant sun, of the Maruts I am Marici, and among the stars I am the moon.

Of the Vedas I am the Sama Veda; of the demigods I am Indra, the king of heaven; of the senses I am the mind; and in living beings I am the living force [consciousness].

Of all the Rudras I am Lord Shiva; of the Yakshas and Rakshasas I am the lord of wealth [Kuvera]; of the Vasus I am fire [Agni], and of the mountains I am Meru.

Of priests, O Arjuna, know Me to be the chief, Brihaspati. Of generals I am Kartikeya, and of bodies of water I am the ocean.

Of the great sages I am Bhrigu; of vibrations I am the transcendental om. Of sacrifices I am the chanting of the holy names [japa], and of immovable things I am the Himalayas.

Of all trees I am the banyan tree, and of the sages among the demigods I am Narada. Of the Gandharvas I am Citraratha, and among perfected beings I am the sage Kapila.

Of horses know Me to be Uchchaihshrava, produced during the churning of the ocean for nectar. Of lordly elephants I am Airavata, and among men I am the monarch.

Of weapons I am the thunderbolt; among cows I am the surabhi. Of causes for reproduction I am Kandarpa, the god of love, and of serpents I am Vasuki.

Of the many-hooded Nagas I am Ananta; and among the aquatics I am the demigod Varuna. Of departed ancestors I am Aryama, and among the dispensers of law I am Yama, lord of death.

Among the Daitya demons I am the devoted Prahlada; among subduers I am time; among beasts I am the lion, and among birds I am Garuda.

Of purifiers I am the wind; of the effective user of weapons I am Rama; of fishes I am the shark, and of flowing rivers I am the Ganges.

Of all creations I am the beginning and the end and also the middle, O Arjuna. Of all sciences I am the spiritual science of the self, and among logicians I am the conclusive truth.

Of letters I am the letter A, and among compound words I am the dual compound. I am also inexhaustible time, and of creators I am Brahma.

I am all-consuming death, and I am the generating principle of all that is yet to be. Among women I am fame, fortune, fine speech, memory, intelligence, determined and patience.

Of the religious songs in the Sama Veda I am Brihat-sama, and of poetry I am the Gayatri. Of months I am Margasirsa [November-December], and of seasons I am flower-bearing spring.

I am also the gambling of cheats, and of the splendid I am the splendor. I am victory, I am adventure, and I am the strength of the strong.

Of the descendants of Vrsni I am Vasudeva, and of the Pandavas I am Arjuna. Of the sages I am Vyasa, and among great thinkers I am Usana.

Among all means of suppressing disregard of law I am punishment, and of those who seek victory I am ethics. Of secret things I am silence, and of the wise I am wisdom.

Furthermore, O Arjuna, I am the generating seed of all existences. There is no being--moving or nonmoving--that can exist without Me.

O mighty conqueror of enemies, there is no end to My divine manifestations. What I have spoken to you is but a mere indication of My infinite opulence.

Know that all opulent, beautiful and glorious creations spring from but a spark of My splendor.

But what need is there, Arjuna, for all this detailed knowledge? With a single fragment of Myself I penetrate and support this entire universe.

Now Let Me Summarize Chapter 10:

Everything originates from Lord Krishna. He is the source of both spiritual and material worlds. Lord Krishna is the supreme cause of all causes and the support and essence of everything. He is present in everyone's heart as the Supersoul. Everything including our body, mind, thoughts and feelings comes from Lord Krishna. Various qualities of living beings are created by Lord Krishna. The devotees are convinced of His divine opulence and spiritual power and thus engage in devotional service and worship Lord Krishna with all their hearts. He is the creator, supporter, and destroyer of all. He is infinite and has no beginning or end. The entire universe is the expansion of a tiny fraction of His energy. Lord Krishna shares in detail about His divine opulence to Arjuna. All wondrous phenomena showing power, beauty, glory, enjoyable, either in the material world or in the spiritual, are but partial evidence of Krishna's divine energies and opulence.

I asked everyone, "Can anyone tell me what do you understand from this chapter?" One participant replied, "Lord is present in everyone's heart as the Supersoul." The other said, "All qualities, body, mind, thoughts and feelings comes from Lord Krishna." One participant asked, "Is there a connection between our body and God?" I said, "Yes there is. Let me explain you.

Take Care Of Your Temple

What would you do if you were given the responsibility to take care of a temple? You will keep it clean. Serve the deity with good food, flowers, water, and leaves. Do prayers regularly. Then why don't you do the same for your own body? Your body is nothing but your very own temple and within it resides God. Keep your body clean with pure and positive thoughts. Serve your body with good food. Listen to your body.

One evening I went out with my family for dinner at a good restaurant on the outskirts of the city, to celebrate my birthday. The restaurant was well kept with good ambience, decor and sitting. We ordered for food and we all were hungry. The food got served and we started eating it. As I took one bite, I felt the taste was not good. Immediately I refused to eat that food item further. My other family members found it okay and had it. Few more food items were served and most of them didn't taste that good and I left that restaurant half empty stomach on my birthday. The very next day all my family members except me complained of food poisoning and had to go to doctor to get treated. One of my cousins asked me, "How come you escaped and we are suffering." I smiled and said, "When my body told me the food doesn't taste good, something is wrong, I listened to it and didn't eat. I used my common sense over my hungry stomach." God is seated within all of us and tells us through our body about what is good and bad for us. So take good care of your temple by eating good food.

A senior employee of a big company was doing good in his career and growing up the corporate ladder very fast. Within a short span of time he reached the position of a Vice President, but he had to pay a price. From a fit man he became an obese old man in no time. His stomach looked similar to that of a pregnant woman. His face was down with dark circles because of excessive smoking. His performance in work started going down. His team was upset because of his over aggressive behavior. He badly needed help. His body kept telling him control your diet, don't stress yourself so much, exercise, go for walks or join gym, reduce weight, sleep well, but he never listened to his body. Until one day he fell unconscious and got admitted to the hospital, only then did he introspect about how much he has ignored his health. From that day till now, he has consciously transformed to a more fitter and younger version of himself. So take good care of your temple by living a healthy life.

I have observed with lots of people around. Whenever they experience any pain or discomfort they avoid going to doctor for a checkup or avoid routine body check up. Isn't it stupid to not listen to our body which shouts loudly in the form of pain, discomfort or when unexpected blood is seen? We know that something is wrong and we need to get ourselves checked with a doctor immediately. God residing within speaks to us saying your body is not functioning properly it needs to be treated. You never know just by being more alert and aware you can save yourself from various diseases, so take good care of your temple by listening to it.

Whenever I get angry, feel low, feel depressed or worry, immediately I come to know that these are nothing but signs of my body saying you are feeling negative. So what do I do? Firstly I recognize that I'm having negative feelings. Secondly, understand why am I feeling negative because of whom or what situation has made me feel negative. Thirdly, immediately replace it with positive thoughts and tune into channel showing positive mental pictures. In the first place we must not let negativity enter our temple, by refusing to see negative in others, by not talking negative about others and keeping distance from people who talk negative and by refusing to listen to negative talks for others as well as for ourselves. So take care of your temple by keeping it clean with pure and positive thoughts.

In the Bhagavad Gita, Lord Krishna told Arjuna that He is present in everyone's heart as the Supersoul. Everything including our body, mind, thoughts and feelings comes from Lord Krishna. Only when you take care of your body by keeping it clean with good positive thoughts, serve it with good food, have good feelings for others and listen to it, only then will you experience Lord Krishna talking with you through your body which is your temple. Here comes another life lesson.

Lesson No: 21 Our body is nothing but our temple in which God resides. Take care of your temple by living healthy, eating good food, thinking positive and listening to it.

After a long time Shikha raised her hand and asked, "What is the connection between heart and God?" I said, "Do you all want to hear another interesting story?" Everyone nodded.

Follow Your Heart

"Once a group of young boys and girls were travelling to a nearby hill station in a bus. They all were having a gala time, drinking and smoking. Lord Krishna wanted to interact with the youth. So Lord Krishna disguised himself as a priest and appeared close to the road where their bus was going to cross and started asking for a lift.

"Hey look there is a priest looking for a lift", said one boy. All the boys and girls somehow agreed to give Him a lift. Lord Krishna smiled and thanked everyone for giving Him a lift till the hill station. Lord Krishna said, "Looks like you all believe in having fun, no interest in God and all but still you stopped gave this priest a lift, it feels good. Thanks."

One girl in the group said, "We have a lot of respect for priests and saints so thought of helping you." Lord Krishna smiled and asked everyone, "Do you believe in God?" One boy said, "Sir we are still so young exploring the world around us and enjoying our youth, at this age who has inclination to even think or believe in God that's for the oldies."

Lord Krishna said, "Would you like to hear an interesting story of God and angels?" Everyone nodded.

"Once God wanted to promote the best angels with an opportunity to serve Him directly at his abode. So He kept a competition and whoever wins will serve God directly. All the angels both male and female were excited and accepted to be a part of this competition. For this they had to take birth as a human and compete on earth. There were approximate 100 angels who took birth as humans on earth. All angels passed through childhood and entered the youth phase of their human form of life. They all were unaware about the fact that they have come to earth for some kind of competition. But the game had already begun.

The first challenge everyone faced was choosing his or her career. Nearly 50 angels failed as they chose that career which others were doing and blindly followed to choose a profession that their friends said or did. Only 50 angels went on the right tack by take up the profession that they liked and enjoyed. They just believed in following their passion.

50 angels who passed the first challenge faced the second challenge. It was to choose the right friends. Nearly 25 angels failed who made friends without using their mind and heart. They just blindly made wrong friends and followed them. Rest 25 were balanced as they used their common sense to make friends whom they really liked and enjoyed being in their company.

Now only 25 angels went ahead for the third challenge. This time challenge was to choose the right life partner. Nearly 13 angels failed to choose the right partner. They just picked up anyone whom they felt attracted to

THE GITA HAPPINESS RETREAT

without understanding how they really feel about their partner. Rest 12 received successes in their relationships by choosing the right partner by fully trusting their vibrations and how they feel when their partner is with them.

12 angels then entered the fourth challenge. It was to become a good human being by help others, forgiving and letting go their ego. Here 6 angels failed to prove themselves in being human. Only 6 succeeded in proving their good nature and attitude by helping everyone in need taking care of their parents, elders, partners needs and also in helping their friends in need.

Now only 6 angels entered the fifth challenge. The challenge was to remain focused on their goals by thinking positive and being optimistic every time. 3 angels failed to stay positive; they failed to control their mind because of which they always thought negative in every situation. Only 3 angels managed to stay, feel and think positive all the time by making a principle in their life to not let negativity of any kind enter their mind.

So finally only 3 angels qualified for the sixth and last challenge. The challenge was who do the angels listens to, their heart or their mind. In that 2 angels failed to follow their heart and became salves of what the head told them to do. There was only 1 angel who blindly trusted and followed what his heart told him to do.

Of course only that 1 angel was promoted to serve God because he consistently did what his heart told him to do. He chose his profession, friends, life partner based on his feelings. He proved himself to being a good human being by thinking and doing things for others from his heart. He was always optimistic about life, blindly trusted and always followed his heart."

After the story narration ended, one boy asked the priest, "What are you trying to say?" Lord Krishna smiled and said, "I totally agree that at this age you want to explore the outer world have fun and enjoy life to the fullest. But this is also the right time to explore your inner world, understand what do you really want, what qualities you have, develop your core values, have a clear understanding of what life is all about, at the same time enjoy life to the fullest, have a right career and amazing relationship with your girlfriend or boyfriend and family, have the insight to choose the right partner for marriage."

Lord Krishna further said, "Do you want to live a life on your own terms or on the terms of destiny? If you want to live and enjoy life to the fullest and not dance to the tunes of destiny then you need to explore within and plan your life in the right direction. No parent or teacher will teach you this. You will come across ups and downs in your life, prepare yourself to deal with it now."

One girl asked, "But how can we take charge of our life?"

Lord Krishna said, "By doing the right things."

Boy asked, "Can you please explain in detail."

Lord Krishna said, "Whatever decisions you take small or big, just place your hand on your heart and ask am I doing the right thing? Is it good for me? Will I be happy by doing this?"

"If the answer you get from within is 'Yes' please go ahead and if your answer is 'No' don't go ahead. If you still feel unsure take help of your parents, teachers or friends who are close to you and then decide."

"Sometimes we are forced to make a hard choice which is against our will or heart and we make that choice under pressure or someone's influence or we happen to get manipulated. Ask yourself will you be happy to do things against your heart just to please someone or the society."

"Immediately stop, look within, follow your heart and it will guide you in the right direction towards right people, right situations and right kind of life."

The bus was filled with silence and everyone was in deep thought trying to understand what the priest just said. It was indeed a great teaching for the young minds to absorb, think and reflect.

But there was one boy who then asked the priest, "Sir what is the connection of God and heart? You are a priest and guiding us to follow our heart."

Lord Krishna smiled and said, "Your Ultimate Guide, Teacher and Friend 'God' is seated in your heart. He is present within each one of you, guiding you every moment."

One boy asked, "How are you so sure about this?"

Priest said, "Lord Krishna stated to Arjuna on the battlefield of Kurukshetra, in the Bhagavad Gita that He is the Supersoul, seated in the hearts of all living entities. He is the Supreme Lord of all the worlds. He is Lord of the Universe. Everything comes from Him."

The entire group was stunned to gain this beautiful insight and thanked the priest for guiding all of them. This brings us to another and very important life lesson.

**Lesson No: 22 God is seated in our hearts. Listen to God's voice within you. Follow your heart.

CHAPTER 11

Arjuna See My Universal Form

"Let's play a game. I want you all to close your eyes and imagine whatever I am saying. Imagine a peacock dancing, a parrot talking, a dog licking your feet, your parents hugging you, you kissing your loved one, a balloon flying high up in the sky. Your eyes have the power to visualize things, events and people even when you keep your eyes closed. Continue to keep your eyes closed; now I want you to imagine the person, people or events, which brings happiness on our face immediately. Now you all can open your eyes and share your happy moments." All participants started sharing their happy moments one by one. "Everyone close your eyes again and now I want you all to imagine the person or event that has hurt you deeply which you couldn't forget till date." There was pin drop silence, everyone closed their eyes and started imagining. "Forgive him or her who has hurt you from your deepest core, right now at this very moment. They might not be here right now or they might have died, still forgive them. Then slowly open your eyes." All the participants were quite as if they experienced something very nice. One participant even started crying and felt light from within that was none other than Shikha. I said, "Our eyes are blessed with the power of visualization, you can use it to create positive happy mental pictures, remember happy moments and you can also forgive people who hurt you and you will see magic happen."

Chapter 11 has 55 shlokas. I request each participant to read two shlokas each that is translated in English." Everyone started reading one after the other.

The Universal Form

Arjuna said: By my hearing the instructions You have kindly given me about these most confidential spiritual subjects, my illusion has now disappeared.

O lotus-eyed one, I have heard from You in detail about the appearance and disappearance of every living entity and have realized Your infinite glories.

O greatest of all personalities, O supreme form, though I see You here before me in Your actual position, as You have described Yourself, I wish to see how You have entered into this cosmic manifestation. I want to see that form of Yours.

If You think that I am able to witness Your cosmic form, O my Lord, O master of all mystic power, then kindly show me that unlimited universal Self.

The Supreme Personality of Godhead said: My dear Arjuna, O son of Pritha, see now My opulence, hundreds of thousands of varied divine and multicolored forms.

O best of the Bharatas, see here the different manifestations of Adityas, Vasus, Rudras, Ashwini-kumaras and all the other demigods. See the many wonderful things which no one has ever seen or heard of before.

O Arjuna, whatever you wish to see, witness at once in this body of Mine! This universal form can show you whatever you now desire to see and whatever you may want to see in the future. Everything— moving and nonmoving--is here completely, in one place.

But you cannot see Me with your present eyes. Therefore I give you divine eyes. See My mystic opulence!

Sanjaya said: O King, having spoken thus, the Supreme Lord of all mystic power, the Personality of Godhead, displayed His universal form to Arjuna.

Arjuna saw in that universal form unlimited mouths, unlimited eyes, unlimited wonderful visions. The form was decorated with many heavenly ornaments and bore many divine upraised weapons. He wore heavenly garlands and garments, and many divine scents were smeared over His body. All was wondrous, brilliant, unlimited, all-expanding.

If hundreds of thousands of suns were to rise at once into the sky, their radiance might resemble the effulgence of the Supreme Person in that universal form.

At that time Arjuna could see in the universal form of the Lord the unlimited expansions of the universe situated in one place although divided into many, many thousands.

Then, confused and astonished, his hair standing on end, Arjuna bowed his head to offer respect and with folded hands began to pray to the Supreme Lord.

Arjuna said: My dear Lord Krishna, I see assembled in Your body all the demigods and various other living entities. I see Brahma sitting on the lotus flower, as well as Lord Shiva and all the sages and divine serpents.

O Lord of the universe, O universal form, I see in Your body many, many arms, bellies, mouths and eyes, expanded everywhere, without limit. I see in You no end, no middle and no beginning.

Your form is difficult to see because of its glaring effulgence, spreading on all sides, like blazing fire or the immeasurable radiance of the sun. Yet I see this glowing form everywhere, decorated with various crowns, clubs and discs.

You are the supreme original objective. You are the ultimate resting place of this entire universe. You are inexhaustible, and You are the oldest. You are the maintainer of the eternal religion, the Personality of Godhead. This is my opinion.

You are without origin, middle or end. Your glory is unlimited. You have numberless arms, and the sun and moon are Your eyes. I see You with blazing fire coming forth from Your mouth, burning this entire universe by Your own radiance.

Although You are one, You spread throughout the sky and the planets and all space between. O great one, seeing this wondrous and terrible form, all the planetary systems are disturbed.

All the hosts of demigods are surrendering before You and entering into You. Some of them, very much afraid, are offering prayers with folded hands. Hosts of great sages and perfected beings, crying "All peace!" are praying to You by singing the Vedic religious songs.

All the various manifestations of Lord Shiva, the Adityas, the Vasus, the Sadhyas, the Visvedevas, the two Ashvins, the Maruts, the forefathers, the Gandharvas, the Yakshas, the Asuras, and the perfected demigods are seeing You in wonder.

O mighty-armed one, all the planets with their demigods are disturbed at seeing Your great form, with its many faces, eyes, arms, thighs, legs and bellies and Your many terrible teeth; and as they are disturbed, so am I.

O all-pervading Vishnu, seeing You with Your many radiant colors touching the sky, Your wide open mouths, and Your great glowing eyes, my mind is worried by fear. I can no longer maintain my steadiness or balance of mind.

O Lord of lords, O refuge of the worlds, please be kind to me. I cannot keep my balance seeing thus Your blazing deathlike faces and awful teeth. In all directions I am puzzled.

All the sons of Dhritarashtra, along with their allied kings, and Bhishma, Drona, Karna--and our chief soldiers also--are rushing into Your fearful mouths. And some I see trapped with heads smashed between Your teeth.

As the many waves of the rivers flow into the ocean, so do all these great warriors enter blazing into Your mouths.

I see all people rushing with full speed into Your mouths, as moths dash to destruction in a blazing fire.

O Vishnu, I see You eating quickly all people from all sides with Your flaming mouths. Covering the entire universe with Your extreme brightness, You are manifest with terrible, scorching rays.

O Lord of lords, so ferocious of form, please tell me who You are. I offer my respect unto You; please be gracious to me. You are the original Lord. I want to know about You, for I do not know what Your mission is.

The Supreme Personality of Godhead said: Time I am, the great destroyer of the worlds, and I have come here to destroy all people. With the exception of you [the Pandavas], all the soldiers here on both sides will be killed.

Therefore get up. Prepare to fight and win glory. Conquer your enemies and enjoy a flourishing kingdom. They are already put to death by My arrangement, and you, O Savyasachi, can be but an instrument in the fight.

Drona, Bhisma, Jayadratha, Karna and the other great warriors have already been destroyed by Me. Therefore, kill them and do not be disturbed. Simply fight, and you will vanquish your enemies in battle.

Sanjaya said to Dhritarashtra: O King, after hearing these words from the Supreme Personality of Godhead, the trembling Arjuna offered respect with folded hands again and again. He fearfully spoke to Lord Krishna in a hesitating voice, as follows:

Arjuna said: O master of the senses, the world becomes joyful upon hearing Your name, and thus everyone becomes attached to You. Although the perfected beings offer You their respectful worship, the demons are afraid, and they flee here and there. All this is rightly done.

O great one, greater even than Brahma, You are the original creator. Why then should they not offer their respectful worship unto You? O limitless one, God of gods, refuge of the universe! You are the indestructible source, the cause of all causes, transcendental to this material manifestation.

You are the original Personality of Godhead, the oldest, the ultimate refuge of this manifested cosmic world. You are the knower of everything, and You are all that is knowable. You are the supreme refuge, above the material modes. O limitless form! This whole cosmic manifestation is present by You!

You are air, You are the supreme controller! You are fire, You are water, and You are the moon! You are Brahma, the first living creature, and You are the great-grandfather. I therefore offer my respectful worship unto You a thousand times, and again and yet again!

Respect to You from the front, from behind and from all sides! O unbounded power, You are the master of limitless might! You are present everywhere, and thus You are everything!

Thinking of You as my friend, I have rashly addressed You "O Krishna," "O Yadava," "O my friend," not knowing Your glories. Please forgive whatever I may have done in madness or in love. I have dishonored You many times, joking as we relaxed, lay on the same bed, or sat or eat together, sometimes alone and sometimes in *front of many friends. O flawless one, please excuse me for all those offenses.*

You are the father of this complete cosmic manifestation, of the moving and the nonmoving. You are its worshipable chief, the supreme spiritual master. No one is equal to You, nor can anyone be one with You. How then could there be anyone greater than You within the three worlds, O Lord of immeasurable power?

You are the Supreme Lord, to be worshiped by every living being. Thus I fall down to offer You my respectful worship and ask Your mercy. As a father tolerates the disrespect of his son, a friend the rudeness of a friend, or a wife the friendliness of her partner, please tolerate the wrongs I may have done You.

After seeing this universal form, which I have never seen before, I am gladdened, but at the same time my mind is disturbed with fear. Therefore please grant Your grace upon me and reveal again Your form as the Personality of Godhead, O Lord of lords, O home of the universe.

O universal form, O thousand-armed Lord, I wish to see You in Your four-armed form, with helmeted head and with club, wheel, conch and lotus flower in Your hands. I long to see You in that form.

The Supreme Personality of Godhead said: My dear Arjuna, happily have I shown you, by My internal power, this supreme universal form within the material world. No one before you has ever seen this original form, unlimited and full of glaring extreme brightness.

O best of the Kuru warriors, no one before you has ever seen this universal form of Mine, for neither by studying the Vedas, nor by performing sacrifices, nor by charity, nor by religious activities, nor by severe self-punishment can I be seen in this form in the material world.

You have been worried and puzzled by seeing this horrible feature of Mine. Now let it be finished. My devotee, be free again from all disturbances. With a peaceful mind you can now see the form you desire.

Sanjaya said to Dhritarashtra: The Supreme Personality of Godhead, Krishna, having spoken thus to Arjuna, displayed His real four-armed form, and at last showed His two-armed form, thus encouraging the fearful Arjuna.

When Arjuna thus saw Krishna in His original form, he said: O Janardana, seeing this humanlike form, so very beautiful, I am now composed in mind, and I am restored to my original nature.

The Supreme Personality of Godhead said: My dear Arjuna, the form of Mine you are now seeing is very difficult to witness. Even the demigods are ever seeking the opportunity to see this form, which is so dear.

The form you are seeing with your transcendental eyes cannot be understood simply by studying the Vedas, nor by undergoing serious self-punishment, nor by charity, nor by worship. It is not by these means that one can see Me as I am.

My dear Arjuna, only by undivided devotional service can I be understood as I am, standing before you, and can thus be seen directly. Only in this way can you enter into the mysteries of My understanding.

My dear Arjuna, he who engages in My pure devotional service, free from the impurities of fruitive activities and mental notion, he who works for Me, who makes Me the supreme goal of his life, and who is friendly to every living being—he certainly comes to Me.

Now Let Me Summarize Chapter 11:

Arjuna expresses his desire to see Lord's Universal form, Lord Krishna then gives Arjuna divine vision and reveals His spectacular unlimited universal form. Lord Krishna thus establishes His divinity as The Supreme Personality of Godhead. Lord Krishna also shows Arjuna the immediate future of what is going to happen on the battlefield, and that his win is confirmed. Lord also confirms that no one has seen this form before. Lord Krishna explains that His own all-beautiful humanlike form is the original form of Godhead. One can realize this form only by pure devotional service.

This also indicates that we cannot see God with our human eyes. We can see Him only through divine vision or trance or Samadhi.

I asked everyone, "Can anyone tell me what do you understand from this chapter?" One participant replied, "We cannot see God with our human eyes, but we can see Him through the power of visualization." Very well said, let's hear more on this.

Magic Will Happen

Imagine one day you got a boon from God. He gifted you with magic eyes with which you can visualize your future and make your wishes come true. Yes it's true, God has actually given us magic eyes it's called the power of visualization.

When I was 10 years old, I was a very stubborn child. If I wanted something I would certainly get it. One day I saw two friends playing video game at their home on TV. I too wanted it and I kept asking for it from my dad and mom again and again. Video games were very new those days, it wasn't available in the market easily and very few had it. You won't believe my uncle from Germany gifted me the same video game Nintendo and I played with it like anything for many years. I never knew that I had the power to visualize and attract things that I wanted badly and they would appear in real. So, when you use magic eyes along with the stubbornness of child magic will happen.

A middle aged married couple was going through rough phase in their married life. They were constantly fighting over petty issues. The understanding and patience was lost between the two. When asked they said we want our marriage to work we just feel helpless when things don't work between us and we don't know what to do. I told them why don't you start visualizing a peaceful relationship with each other. Think of the great times you had with each other in past. Think of the times when you went out for vacations, partying, for movies and experienced those amazing moments. Consciously try to visualize your beautiful past and think what all you wish to do in future together. Set love goals say for example if your wife wishes to learn swimming at this age instead of discouraging her both of you join swimming lessons and work together to fulfill each other's love goals. In no time the moment you start accomplishing your love goals magic will happen.

Today more and more people are using their magic eyes to fulfill their dreams. Be it a sportsperson, an actor, an entrepreneur, a job seeker, a businessman, a scientist, a housewife and many more. "Decide what you want, believe you can have it, believe you deserve it. Then close your eyes everyday for few minutes and visualize having what you really want, feel you have already received it. Be grateful for having it and enjoy it. Trust that the Universe will figure out how to manifest it." These are the words said in the famous book "The Secret" written by Rhonda Byrne.

In the Bhagavad Gita, on the battlefield of Kurukshetra, Lord Krishna gave divine eyes to Arjuna to see Lord's Universal form. This means that we need divine eyes or magic eyes to see God. When we close our human eyes, our divine eyes or magic eyes gets activated through the power of visualization and with God's blessings we can see God within ourselves. Now you know why do we close our eyes while praying. Use your magic eyes to manifest whatever you desire, to forgive people, to achieve love goals, to see God and magic will happen. This brings us to another life lesson.

Lesson No: 23 God has given us divine eyes or magic eyes. With the power of visualization you can get whatever you desire. Use divine eyes or magic eyes to forgive people in your past. With divine eyes or magic eyes you can see God within yourself.

One participant raised his hand and asked, "In this chapter Lord showed His Universal form to Arjuna, but why didn't Lord stop the Kurukshetra war from happening?" Another participant said, "There are so many crimes happening in this world, why is God not stopping it from happening?" Let's hear this interesting conversation between Lord Krishna and Arjuna.

I Am The Greatest Proof

Once Arjuna just happened to ask Lord Krishna, "My dearest friend, why did You show Your Universal form to me just before the onset of the war?" Lord Krishna said, "You had asked me that's why I showed you." Arjuna said, "But You could have easily avoided." Lord Krishna smiled and said, "Arjuna this was My way to prove to you and the world that I exist and that I am the Original Supreme Personality of Godhead. Without showing My Universal form, people won't believe that I am God and it was also required to build faith in my devotees."

Arjuna asked, "Then Lord You could have easily stopped the Kurukshetra war from happening, but why didn't You?" Lord Krishna said, "Arjuna you are right, I do have the power to stop such happenings. But, My job is to guide everyone to the right direction that can change one's destiny but people refuse to listen."

Arjuna said, "Lord in this modern world crimes like domestic violence, marital rape, physical assault, verbal abuse and what not is happening behind closed doors. Why are women and even men suffering refuse to talk about it, they do not take a step to run away from it, report it to police or seek help?" Lord Krishna replied, "It's fear, what will the society say, my parents won't understand and help me, how will I manage myself all alone in future, nobody will believe that being a man I am facing verbal abuse from my wife. Everyone curses Me as to why did I put them in such a grave situation. They loose belief in Me and never ask for My help."

Arjuna said, "It's true if a noble soul and believer in God faces such situations they will certainly loose faith in themselves and You. But what's the solution to it?"

Lord Krishna replied, "Just like Kurukshetra war, each and every human being will have to fight his own war. Sometimes with his own mind, sometimes with people close to them and sometimes with society. They have to say a firm No and refuse to bear any ill treatment done to them. As God my job is not to stop the war from happening but to guide every soul in doing what is right, helping him or her in taking the right action at the right time so that they can put an end to their sufferings. But problem is people loose faith in Me and curse Me instead of listening to Me. I shout from deep within each of them to either run or call or seek help, I show them the direction but they feel so afraid that they just refuse to act."

Lord Krishna further said, "There are times when people blackmail or on gun point force you to do things which you don't want to do. At that time one should not bear any ill treatment, have firm belief in Me and take action in right direction without worrying what if he or she discloses my secrets to the world or what if he or she kills me. Be fearless and refuse to budge.

Today there are a lot of incidents happening where guys are taking obscene pictures of girls they are obsessed about and threating them to disclose their videos to the world so that they loose face in society and their self confidence is finished. Any girl or women would feel shit scared. Fear is what they are taking advantage of. The day you believe that I 'God' exists in this world and within you. The day you have confidence in Me that whenever I call my Lord He will certainly help me. That day that moment you become fearless. Your fearlessness is My greatest proof of existence."

In the Bhagavad Gita, Lord Krishna showed Arjuna His Universal form giving proof to him and the world that He is the Supreme Personality of Godhead and teaches us another important life lesson.

**Lesson No: 24 Lord Krishna is indeed the Supreme Personality of Godhead, which He has proved to the world by showing his Universal form. The day you believe that God exists in this world that moment you become fearless.

CHAPTER 12

Worship Me With Full Devotion

"It's time to use your note pad again. 25 years back was the time when writing letters was very common before email came in. Today we will go back in time and write letters to our loved ones. Those of you who are single can write a letter to your parents or anyone who is close to you. Objective of this exercise is to express our love for those who matter to us. There is no compulsion to send this letter to them but writing is important. Time is 5 minutes.

Okay times up. Any volunteers who want to share their love letter with all of us please come forward." Three participants came forward and shared their letters and the entire room was filled with positive happy vibrations of love.

It's time to move to the next chapter. There are 20 Shlokas in Chapter 12 of The Bhagavad Gita. I request each participant to read one shloka each that is translated in English." Everyone started reading one after the other.

Devotional Service

Arjuna inquired: Which is considered to be more perfect, those who are always properly engaged in Your devotional service, or those who worship the impersonal Brahman, the Absolute, pure and formless being?

The Supreme Personality of Godhead said: Those who fix their minds on My personal form and are always engaged in worshiping Me with great and transcendental faith are considered by Me to be most perfect.

But those who fully worship the Absolute pure formless being, that which lies beyond the awareness of the senses, the all-pervading, unimaginable, unchanging, fixed and immovable-the impersonal conception of the Absolute Truth-by controlling the various senses and being equally inclined to everyone, such persons, engaged in the welfare of all, at last achieve Me.

For those whose minds are attached to the Absolute pure formless being, impersonal feature of the Supreme, advancement is very troublesome. To make progress in that discipline is always difficult for those who are embodied.

But those who worships Me, giving up all their activities unto Me and being devoted to Me without deviation, engaged in devotional service and always meditating upon Me, having fixed their minds upon Me, O son of Pritha--for them I am the swift deliverer from the ocean of birth and death.

Just fix your mind upon Me, the Supreme Personality of Godhead, and engage all your intelligence in Me. Thus you will live in Me always, without a doubt.

My dear Arjuna, O winner of wealth, if you cannot fix your mind upon Me without deviation, then follow the regulated principles of bhakti-yoga. In this way you will develop a desire to attain to Me.

If you cannot practice the regulations of bhakti-yoga, then just try to work for Me, because by working for Me you will come to the perfect stage.

If, however, you are unable to work in this consciousness of Me, then try to act giving up all results of your work and try to be self-situated.

If you cannot take to this practice, then engage yourself in the cultivation of knowledge. Better than knowledge, however, is meditation, and better than meditation is giving up the fruits of action, for by such giving up one can attain peace of mind.

One who is not jealous but is a kind friend to all living entities, who does not think himself a proprietor and is free from false ego, who is equal in both happiness and distress, who is tolerant, always satisfied, self-controlled, and engaged in devotional service with determination, his mind and intelligence fixed on Me—such a devotee of Mine is very dear to Me.

He for whom no one is put into difficulty and who is not disturbed by anyone, who is balanced in happiness and distress, fear and anxiety, is very dear to Me.

My devotee who is not dependent on the ordinary course of activities, who is pure, expert, without cares, free from all pains, and not striving for some result, is very dear to Me.

One who neither rejoices nor grieves, who neither complaints nor desires, and who rejects both auspicious and inauspicious things— such a devotee is very dear to Me.

One who is equal to friends and enemies, who is balanced in honor and dishonor, heat and cold, happiness and distress, fame and disgrace, who is always free from contaminating association, always silent and satisfied with anything, who doesn't care for any residence, who is fixed in knowledge and who is engaged in devotional service— such a person is very dear to Me.

Those who follow this everlasting path of devotional service and who completely engage themselves with faith, making Me the supreme goal, are very, very dear to Me.

Let Me Now Summarize Chapter 12:

Arjuna asks Lord Krishna about devotee engaged in pure devotional service and devotee of impersonal Brahman, who is perfect? Of which Lord Krishna says Bhakti-yoga, pure devotional service to Lord Krishna, is the highest and most convenient means for attaining pure love for Krishna. Those who follow this supreme path develop divine qualities. This path consists of daily deity worship, offering fruits and flowers, singing religious songs in praise of the glory of Krishna. This can be achieved by fixing his mind upon Krishna without deviation. Lord also mentioned other ways of reaching to him by working for Krishna, or by giving up results of his work, or through knowledge or meditation or by giving up fruits of action.

I asked everyone, "Can anyone tell me what do you understand from this chapter?" One participant replied, "It talks about devotional service where bhakti yoga is considered the highest and best way to love Lord Krishna." Another participant said, "Bhakti is exactly how many people pray in their homes and temples." One participant asked, "Madam how is devotional service connected with the love letter exercise?" I said, "I knew this is coming. Listen carefully.

Unconditional Love

Have you ever fallen in love with someone?

Have you fallen in love with the same person multiple times?

That's Unconditional Love.

Loving that one person when the conditions are not right. When he or she is rude, angry, unfaithful, imperfect, upset, sad, uncaring, ungrateful, forgetful and crazy. But you still say, "Come what may I will always love you." That's true love.

A young man and a young woman were best of friends. They loved each other, cared for one another, had lot of respect for each other and trusted each other. Then one day, their love went through troubled waters. The young woman happened to go out with some other male friend and unknowingly happened to have a physical relationship with him. The young man felt uncomfortable from within and questioned her about what happened? The young woman didn't want to lie and spoke the truth about what happened that night. The young man was deeply hurt. Then he too went ahead and shared a physical relationship with another woman, may be out of frustration.

What do you think could have happened to their friendship and relationship?

Well they both forgave each other and continued with their unconditional love for each other. Their love was tested many a times by trespassers provoking them to cross their lines and create unrest in their relationship. Some trespassers were successful, but their love for each other was so strong that they themselves couldn't break their bond. Every time they were knocked down both of them came back together and said to each other, "Come what may I will always love you."

When I was 25 years old, someone asked me what kind of a guy do you want to get married to and why?

I told her I want to get married to a guy who will love me unconditionally. Just the way my father loved my mother till her last breath. My mother was on wheelchair for 4 years, she was paraplegic. My father and my mother had a tough time dealing with this unfortunate incident but their unconditional love kept them going. My father always said to my mother, "Come what may I will always love you."

Have you ever loved yourself?

Few years back I was frequently feeling low, depressed and sad. I wanted to come out of this problem. So one day my heart told me, "Sheetal why don't you write down all the things that you love doing". I said, "That's a good idea". You won't believe. I made a list of 50 things that I love doing. Like go for shopping, watch a funny movie, call your best friend and talk, meet your best friend for coffee or dinner, go to a spa, go for vacation and many more. Now I tell myself, "Come what may I will always love myself."

Lord Krishna had also mentioned to Arjuna in the Bhagavad Gita, that those who follow this everlasting path of devotional service (Unconditional love for Me) and who completely engage themselves with faith, making Me the supreme goal, are very, very dear to Me. Today we all are so busy, sometimes falling in love sometimes falling out of love. But how many of us actually love God. Whenever we go to the temple and pray, we ask God for something or the other. When we go through tough problems, we ask God why me. But have you ever told God that, "Come what may I will always love You." So be it Lord Krishna or your loved one or your best friend or your partner or yourself just say to them, "Come what may I will always love you unconditionally."

Lesson No: 25 Love your partner, loved one, best friend Unconditionally. Love yourself Unconditionally. Love Lord Krishna Unconditionally.

One participant raised his hand and asked, "Why do devotees suffer, why is that even the devotees of Lord have to face challenges in life?" Another participant said, "You mentioned about your mother on wheelchair, how can a person love God when he suffers to this extent?" To answer this, there is a conversation that takes place between Lord Krishna and Goddess Laxmi. Let's hear it.

The Challenges

One day Goddess Lakshmi and Lord Vishnu were sitting and discussing in general. When Goddess Lakshmi enquired, "Lord why is it that your devotees have to undergo so many challenges in human form of life? Even if some pure soul becoming your greatest devotee still he faces challenges in his life, he always looks up and says God why did you do this to me?"

Lord Vishnu said, "Challenges are part and parcel of life. What is life without challenges? Don't you think life will become boring if there were no ups and downs?"

"The challenges are nothing but tests sent by Me every now and then. To check his or her level of devotion towards Me and also his or her true love for Me and whenever he or she passes the test with flying colors it makes Me feel good. In human life too, whenever my devotee comes across challenges in personal life, relationships, work life or in achieving goals it becomes important to develop an attitude to overcome it rather than run away, give up or get bogged down from it. Remember where ever there is a problem there is also a solution. In fact whenever my devotee faces challenges I help him, guide him, show him the direction and provide solution to overcome that challenge."

Goddess Lakshmi said, "What about those devotees who face a grave challenge of having physical disabilities wherein they become dependent forever."

Lord Vishnu said, "Let me share a conversation that happened when I met a person having physical disability. When I looked at him I felt like immediately using my powers to heal him. But unfortunately it was his past bad karmas because of which he was suffering in this state.

I asked him, "Don't you get angry at God when you suffer every moment?" That person replied, "I do feel angry and do feel the pain. But when you accept it as part of your life and look for solutions there is a lot than we can do to improve our life. Today if God hasn't given me legs to walk no worries but He gave someone the power to develop artificial limbs to make our lives better. Today if God hasn't given someone eyes to see, he has made technology so advance that with an eye transplant one can get back to a normal life. Today if someone is declared disabled for life, God has given a loving family to take care of. Today we have work from home options and there are many companies open to recruiting people like us. I thank all those companies who have prepared apps to order food at home and send cabs at home that have made our lives so easy. Our life will only change when we accept the unfortunate, seek for forgiveness and surrender to God for a solution. Blaming God will not change our lives but loving Him with full devotion can make the impossible truly possible. Never stop praying and never loose hope."

Lord Krishna further said to Goddess Lakshmi, "A person belonging to LGBT community also faces challenges to a great extent. First in understanding his true nature, real self and secondly in accepting themselves as the way they are. The entire world has accepted them but have they accepted the way they are and come to terms of how they feel? There are many people from this community who have overcome this challenge and made a name for them in society."

Lord Krishna said, "For Me all My devotees are equal. I personally take care of them.

In the Bhagavad Gita I mentioned about two paths of bhakti (devotional service) to Arjuna. One is a straight the ultimate short cut path where my devotee worships Me with full faith, he has no doubts, he is fully committed, fully engaged and loves me unconditionally. My devotee is someone whose only goal is to reach Me even though he prays and has respect for other demigods, he is loyal to Me only and considers Me as his ultimate goal. Even if he faces most dangerous of challenges still his faith is not deviated that's the true quality of my devotee. The second path is filled with twists and turns where in my devotee thinks of Me as formless and impersonal Brahman and worships Me that way. It's not wrong but that path is not the short cut to reach Me. This path has its own challenges but ultimately the devotee reaches Me." This teaches us another life lesson.

Lesson No: 26 The most easiest path to reach God is the path of worship and prayer. The love of God is called devotion (Bhakti). To a true devotee God gives the knowledge and understanding of the Self.

It was 12 and everyone was looking at their watch. "I know its 12, we will now have a short tea break and come back at 12.20 pm.

CHAPTER 13

Real Knowledge

Everyone was seated after coming back from a short tea break. "It's show time. I want you all to have a look at the trailer of famous Bollywood movie "Kick". I am sure everyone must have watched this movie." Everyone nodded. "We will talk about this movie a little later.

It's time for the next chapter. There are 35 Shlokas in Chapter 13 of The Bhagavad Gita. I request each participant to read one shloka each that is translated in English." Everyone started reading one after the other.

Nature, the Enjoyer, and Consciousness

Arjuna said: O my dear Krishna, I wish to know about prakriti [nature], Purusha [the enjoyer], and the field and the knower of the field, and of knowledge and the object of knowledge. The Supreme Personality of Godhead said: This body, O son of Kunti, is called the field, and one who knows this body is called the knower of the field.

O descendant of Bharata, you should understand that I am also the knower in all bodies, and to understand this body and its knower is called knowledge. That is My opinion.

Now please hear My brief description of this field of activity and how it is created, what its changes are, whence it is produced, who that knower of the field of activities is, and what his influences are.

That knowledge of the field of activities and of the knower of activities is described by various sages in various Vedic writings. It is especially presented in the Vedanta-sutra with all reasoning as to cause and effect.

The five great elements, false ego, intelligence, the unmanifested, the ten senses and the mind, the five sense objects, desire, hatred, happiness, sorrow, the whole, the life symptoms, and believes-all these are considered, in summary, to be the field of activities and its interactions.

Humility; pridelessness; nonviolence; tolerance; simplicity; approaching a bona fide spiritual master; cleanliness; steadiness; self-control; giving up of the objects of sense satisfaction; absence of false ego; the perception of the evil of birth, death, old age and disease; detachment; freedom from involvement with children, wife, home and the rest; even-mindedness amid pleasant and unpleasant events; constant and pure devotion to Me; aspiring to live in a solitary place; detachment from the general mass of people; accepting the importance of self-realization; and philosophical search for the Absolute Truth--all these I declare to be knowledge, and besides this whatever there may be is ignorance.

I shall now explain the knowable, knowing which you will taste the eternal. Brahman, the spirit, beginningless and subordinate to Me, lies beyond the cause and effect of this material world.

Everywhere are His hands and legs, His eyes, heads and faces, and He has ears everywhere. In this way the Supersoul exists, being present in everything.

The Supersoul is the original source of all senses, yet He is without senses. He is unattached, although He is the maintainer of all living beings. He is beyond the modes of nature, and at the same time He is the master of all modes of material nature.

The Supreme Truth exists outside and inside of all living beings, the moving and the nonmoving. Because He is so minute, He is beyond the power of the material senses to see or to know. Although far, far away, He is also near to all.

Although the Supersoul appears to be divided among all beings, He is never divided. He is situated as one. Although He is the maintainer of every living entity, it is to be understood that He destroys and develops all.

He is the source of light in all luminous objects. He is beyond the darkness of matter and is unmanifested. He is knowledge, He is the object of knowledge, and He is the goal of knowledge. He is situated in everyone's heart.

Thus the field of activities [the body], knowledge, and the knowable have been summarily described by Me. Only My devotees can understand this thoroughly and thus attain to My nature.

Material nature and the living entities should be understood to be beginningless. Their transformations and the modes of matter are products of material nature.

Nature is said to be the cause of all material causes and effects, whereas the living entity is the cause of the various sufferings and enjoyments in this world.

The living entity in material nature thus follows the ways of life, enjoying the three modes of nature. This is due to his association with that material nature. Thus he meets with good and evil amongst various species.

Yet in this body there is another, a transcendental enjoyer, who is the Lord, the supreme proprietor, who exists as the overseer and permitter, and who is known as the Supersoul.

One who understands this philosophy concerning material nature, the living entity and the interaction of the modes of nature is sure to attain freedom. He will not take birth here again, regardless of his present position.

Some become aware of the Supersoul within themselves through meditation, others through the cultivation of knowledge, and still others through working without fruitive desires.

Again there are those who, although not familiar in spiritual knowledge, begin to worship the Supreme Person upon hearing about Him from others. Because of their tendency to hear from authorities, they also transcend the path of birth and death.

O chief of the Bharatas, know that whatever you see in existence, both the moving and the nonmoving, is only a combination of the field of activities and the knower of the field.

One who sees the Supersoul accompanying the individual soul in all bodies, and who understands that neither the soul nor the Supersoul within the destructible body is ever destroyed, actually sees.

One who sees the Supersoul equally present everywhere, in every living being, does not degrade himself by his mind. Thus he approaches the transcendental destination.

One who can see that all activities are performed by the body, which is created of material nature, and sees that the self does nothing, actually sees.

When a sensible man stops to see different identities due to different material bodies and he sees how beings are expanded everywhere, he attains to the Brahman conception.

Those with the vision of everlasting life can see that the imperishable soul is transcendental, eternal, and beyond the modes of nature. Despite contact with the material body, O Arjuna, the soul neither does anything nor is entangled.

The sky, due to its fine nature, does not mix with anything, although it is present everywhere. Similarly, the soul situated in Brahman vision, does not mix with the body, though situated in that body.

O son of Bharata, as the sun alone illuminates this entire universe, so does the living entity, one within the body, illuminate the entire body by consciousness.

Those who see with eyes of knowledge this difference between the body and the knower of the body, and can also understand the process of freedom from bondage in material nature, attain to the supreme goal.

Let Me Now Summarize Chapter 13:

Arjuna asked Lord Krishna to tell him about nature, enjoyer, body, knower of the body, knowledge and the object of knowledge. Lord Krishna explained in detail about material nature, the soul who is the enjoyer and suffer when it comes in contact with three modes of material nature, the body and Supersoul. Lord Krishna also explained to Arjuna about knowledge, one who understands the difference between the body, the soul and the Supersoul which is beyond modes of nature attains freedom from this material world and will not take birth here again regardless of his present situation. The Supersoul is the object of knowledge and is situated in everyone's heart.

I asked everyone, "Can anyone tell me what do you understand from this chapter?" One participant replied, "Material nature is our physical body, the enjoyer and suffer is the soul and Consciousness is the Supersoul." "Fantastic", was my instant answer. Another participant said, "In this chapter Lord Krishna explained to Arjuna was is real knowledge." One participant said, "Madam we all are curious to know how this chapter is linked with the movie Kick." I smiled and said, "Listen carefully.

Kick

Do you remember what gave Salman Khan kick in his movie "Kick"?

When he helped needy children with money for their medical treatment that's what gave him a kick.

Do you know what gives me a kick? The Bhagavad Gita. When I write and talk about it and how it can help solve problems, that's what gives me a kick.

There are two types of Kick one experiences. The kick you get which knocks you down and the kick you feel within.

Have you ever felt mentally drained and stressed while taking a decision? Have you felt confused and restless when it comes to making the right decision? Do you constantly worry about the decisions you have taken? We all face these situations every now and then and we constantly worry, cause one wrong decision can kick us down.

Here is the solution: Take decisions with the help of a kick list. Now, what's a kick list? Kick list is nothing but set of principles based on your core values and true self.

Many years back as an entrepreneur, I used to constantly worry about my work. Sometimes business acquisition issues, sometimes delivery issues and most of the times employees issues. I used to feel kick down with work stress. So I asked my friend who is also into business for help. He told me, "You need to make decision based on certain Principles." I said, "What do you mean by Principles?" He said, "It is a rule book that you need to follow religiously in your professional life and in your personal life." So I said to him, "Can you share an example?" To that he said, "Its very simple, if you want to maintain a balance in your professional life and personal life and give time to both. Make it a rule not to work on Sundays at all come what may either complete your office work on Saturday or do it on Monday. Take a break." He further said, "I do not bring my work at home. I make sure I complete my work at my office itself and give my 100% attention to my family when I am home. This is one of the rules I follow." He said, "You can keep on adding as many rules as possible, like I am very particular to reach to my client meetings 15 minutes before time and so on…" So set your principles right and follow your kick list religiously.

Many years back a woman whom I know very well had placed her profile at one of the leading newspaper on their matrimonial page. A gang portraying to be sophisticated high class people reverted to her profile showing keen interest. The talks went on smoothly and were much faster than she even expected. Slowly, when the time to meet came they made up stories and conned her emotionally and financially. After that incident she made it a rule that she will not get emotionally involved with any unknown person. Incident like this kicks down one's confidence level that's the time when you should learn from your mistakes and set boundaries to never let anyone take advantage of you. Set your ground rules right and make your own kick list.

Today we all are surrounded by lots of motivational videos, texts, images and stories of wisdom thanks to social media. But what do we do about it, just press like button, share it or forward it to our family and friends then forget about it. Here is what I want you to do, prepare a Kick list. I have prepared a Kick list in which I have listed all the pieces of wisdom, good things which relate with my core values and things that I should not do which are against my true nature. So whenever I get kicked down in life I immediately refer to my kick list and follow it. I urge you all to prepare and religiously follow your kick list, which will bring you all the success, happiness and peace in your life.

Many successful people religiously follow their own set of rules. When we set rules it needs to be in alignment with our body, heart and conscious. We set rules to become wise decision makers. In the Bhagavad Gita, Lord Krishna helped Arjuna to come out of confusion and take the right decision. Lord Krishna told Arjuna about his nature is that of a warrior and quitting this war is not the right thing to do. Lord Krishna even told about the Supersoul who is seated in everyone's heart next to the individual soul, who is guiding us all the time. Lord Krishna gave Arjuna the knowledge about nature, soul and Supersoul with which he can decide and act on what he feels is right. Similarly, we need to make decisions based on what's our true nature, what our heart tells us to do and do it with full consciousness. So make your own kick list, trust it and follow it religiously boldly and blindly. This brings us another very important life lesson.

**Lesson No: 27 Take decisions based on your Principles. Make your own kick list, trust it and follow it religiously, boldly and blindly. Make

decisions based on your true nature, what your heart tells you to do and do it with full consciousness.

After a long time Shikha raised her hand and asked, "Women face a lot of challenges in life, especially went it comes to work, what do you have to say about it?" I totally agree with you, there is an interesting story of Lord Krishna wanting to help women. Let's hear it.

Women In Trouble

One day Lord Krishna was very upset. He was moving from one corner to the other. So his assistant came up to Him and asked, "God what happened, why are you so upset?" Lord Krishna said, "My most beautiful creation on earth 'women' are not happy, they are constantly in a state of worry." His assistant asked, "But what's the worry?" Lord Krishna said, "They are confused all the time and are not able to take the right decision because of which they fall in trouble." His assistant further said, "What can we do about it?" Lord Krishna said, "We can surely guide them." His assistant asked, "But how?"

So Lord Krishna disguised Himself as a woman and joined a group of four women who were discussing their personal issues. One woman said, "It's becoming a constant challenge for me to do recruitment business. I need to meet new clients to generate business. Recently an HR Manager of a very big company was interested in giving me business of doing recruitments worth lakhs, he even showed me where to get the data of right candidates free of cost, he even told me that I just need to talk and schedule those candidates for interview with him. All he wanted was a commission for selecting candidates from the fees that will be paid to me from the company. I really did not understand what to do in this case."

Second woman who is in the sales profession said, "You are lucky this client is just asking you for commission. In my case when I go to acquire fresh business for my company, they directly ask for sexual favors in return. I am equally stuck as to what to do."

Third woman said, "I work as an assistant to the Director of a company. Here my boss is asking for sexual relationship else he will hire someone else and fire me from my job."

Fourth woman who is working in a finance company said, "I am forced to create fake reports and documents. I too feel stuck all the time."

The fifth woman who was Lord Krishna was listening to their conversation patiently and said, "Look I know I am new here but can I suggest something." Rest of the women nodded. So the fifth woman said, "You will always come across difficult situations in your life, may be at work or at home. All we need to do is identify the right and the wrong path. Sometimes we are forced to take the wrong path because of the fear of loosing something. But tell me isn't our integrity bigger and more powerful. You just need to choose the right path in every situation based on your values and leave the rest to God."

The fifth woman looked at the first woman and said, "If you find it okay to give commission to that HR Manager who is asking for it in an unethical way cheating his own employer, then go ahead. Else you have the capability of getting business from so many other companies. Why work with this one. Choice is certainly yours."

The fifth woman looked at the second woman and said, "Ask yourself many times, should I accept that client's offer of sexual favor in exchange of business. Will I get happiness with that business which will come from the wrong way? If the answer you get is No, then why do it. Stop, look for business elsewhere. Now you know why #Metoo has become such a big movement. Think before you act."

The fifth woman looked at the third woman and said, "If you get scared now you will never be confident about yourself and take decisions in life. The very fact that you are discussing with us means you know whatever your boss is asking is not right. Why work with such a person in the first place who will keep on demanding for sex. Your friend who is a recruitment consultant will help you get a new job. When your heart says someone is not right, it is always right."

The fifth woman looked at the fourth woman and said, "When you do some work consciously and you know it's not right. You will not be able to sleep in the night, that thought will keep on disturbing you and your health. Our body, which has mind and senses, it gives us knowledge of the right and wrong. Our heart continuously tells us to choose the right path. Only when our body, heart and conscious are in alignment with each other, then we shall be able to experience true happiness and peace."

In the end, the fifth woman looked at everyone and said, "In the Bhagavad Gita, Lord Krishna had also explained to Arjuna that due to the association of human beings with nature, they shall meet with good and evil amongst various species. The human beings themselves are the very cause of the various sufferings and enjoyments in this world. This happens because of each and every decision they make. In this human body there is another, a transcendental enjoyer, who is the Lord, the supreme proprietor, who exists as the overseer and permitter, and who is known as the Supersoul. One who sees the Supersoul accompanying the individual soul in all bodies, and who understands that neither the soul nor the Supersoul within the destructible body is ever destroyed, actually sees. Those who see with eyes of knowledge by being full consciousness this difference between the body and the knower of the body that's Supersoul, and can also understand the process of freedom from the bondage of suffering in material nature, attain to the supreme goal." This teaches us another life lesson.

**Lesson No: 28 Whenever you face difficult situation, Stop and Think before you act. Decide and choose the right path in every situation based on your values and leave the rest to God. The Right path is when your body, heart and conscious are in alignment with each other.

CHAPTER 14

What is Goodness, Passion And Ignorance?

"Whose favorite actor is Shahid Kapoor? Nice to see few hands up. It's show time again. I want you all to have a look at the trailer of his famous super hit movies, "Kabir Singh", "Badmaash Company" and "Vivah". I am sure everyone must have watched these movies." Everyone nodded. "We will talk about the correlation of these movies with Chapter 14 later.

It's time for the next chapter. There are 27 Shlokas in Chapter 14 of The Bhagavad Gita. I request each participant to read one shloka each that is translated in English." Everyone started reading one after the other.

The Three Modes of Material Nature

The Supreme Personality of Godhead said: Again I shall declare to you this supreme wisdom, the best of all knowledge, knowing which all the sages have attained to supreme perfection.

By becoming fixed in this knowledge, one can attain to the transcendental nature like My own. Thus established, one is not born at the time of creation nor disturbed at the time of dissolution.

The total material substance, called Brahman, is the source of birth, and it is that Brahman that I impregnate, making possible the births of all living beings, O son of Bharata.

It should be understood that all species of life, O son of Kunti, are made possible by birth in this material nature, and that I am the seed-giving father.

Material nature consists of the three modes-goodness, passion and ignorance. When the eternal living entity comes in contact with nature, O mighty-armed Arjuna, he becomes controlled by these modes.

O sinless one, the mode of goodness, being purer than the others, is illuminating, and it frees one from all sinful reactions. Those situated in that mode become conditioned by a sense of happiness and knowledge.

The mode of passion is born of unlimited desires and longings, O son of Kunti, and because of this the embodied living entity is bound to material fruitive actions.

O son of Bharata, know that the mode of darkness, born of ignorance, is misleading all embodied living entities. The results of this mode are madness, inactivity, laziness and sleep, which bind the conditioned soul.

O son of Bharata, the mode of goodness conditions one to happiness; passion conditions one to fruitive action; and ignorance, covering one's knowledge, binds one to madness.

Sometimes the mode of goodness becomes prominent, defeating the mode of passion and ignorance, O son of Bharata. Sometimes the mode of passion defeats goodness and ignorance, and at other times ignorance defeats goodness and passion. In this way there is always competition for supremacy.

The presence of the mode of goodness can be experienced when all the gates of the body are illuminated by knowledge.

O chief of the Bharatas, when there is an increase in the mode of passion the symptoms of great attachment, fruitive activity, intense effort, and uncontrollable desire and strong wish develop.

When there is an increase in the mode of ignorance, O son of Kuru, darkness, inactivity, madness and false belief are seen.

When one dies in the mode of goodness, he attains to the pure higher planets of the great sages.

When one dies in the mode of passion, he takes birth among those engaged in fruitive activities; and when one dies in the mode of ignorance, he takes birth in the animal kingdom.

The result of religious action is pure and is said to be in the mode of goodness. But action done in the mode of passion result in sadness and action performed in the mode of ignorance result in foolishness.

From the mode of goodness, real knowledge develops; from the mode of passion, greed develops; and from the mode of ignorance, develops foolishness, madness and false belief.

Those situated in the mode of goodness gradually go upward to the higher planets; those in the mode of passion live on the earthly planets; and those in the inferior mode of ignorance go down to the hellish worlds.

When one properly sees that in all activities no other performer is at work than these modes of nature and he knows the Supreme Lord, who is transcendental to all these modes, he attains My spiritual nature.

When the embodied being is able to transcend these three modes associated with the material body, he can become free from birth, death, old age and their distresses and can enjoy nectar even in this life.

Arjuna inquired: O my dear Lord, by which symptoms is one known who is transcendental to those three modes? What is his behavior? And how does he transcend the modes of nature?

The Supreme Personality of Godhead said: O son of Pandu, he who does not hate illumination, attachment and misunderstanding when they are present or long for them when they disappear; who is unwavering and undisturbed through all these reactions of the material qualities, remaining neutral and transcendental, knowing that the modes alone are active; who is situated in the self and regards alike happiness and sorrow; who looks upon a lump of earth, a stone and a piece of gold with an equal eye; who is equal toward the desirable and the undesirable; who is steady, situated equally well in praise and blame, honor and dishonor; who treats alike both friend and enemy; and who has given up all material activities--such a person is said to have transcended the modes of nature.

One who engages in full devotional service, unfailing in all circumstance, at once transcends the modes of material nature and thus comes to the level of Brahman.

And I am the basis of the impersonal Brahman, which is immortal, imperishable and eternal and is the fundamental position of ultimate happiness.

Let Me Now Summarize Chapter 14:

Lord Krishna gives knowledge to Arjuna as to how anyone can attain transcendental (spiritual) nature like Him. All living beings come under the control of the three modes of material nature: goodness, passion and ignorance. Lord Krishna explained what these modes are, how they act upon us, how one can transcends them. Lord also explained the symptoms of one who has attained the transcendental state. When one properly sees that all work is done by these three modes of nature and that we are not the doers, actually sees. But we are responsible for our actions because we are given a mind and free will to decide and choose between right and wrong action. You can escape from the influence of three modes of material nature by making a sincere effort by engaging in devotional service to Lord Krishna. When a living being is able to transcend the three modes associated with the material body, he becomes free from birth, death, old age and their distresses and can be happy even in this life.

I asked everyone, "Can anyone tell me what do you understand from this chapter?" One participant replied, "We are under the spell of the three modes of material nature: goodness, passion and ignorance and Lord Krishna guides us how to go beyond it." "Superb", was my instant answer. Another participant said, "We are responsible for our actions and can escape from the influence of the three modes by engaging in devotional service to Lord Krishna." One participant said, "Madam Shahid Kapoor is my favorite actor and I want to know how this chapter is linked with his movies." I smiled and said, "Listen carefully.

Which Path Will You Walk On?

We are faced with numerous challenges in our day-to-day life. How can we overcome them? By choosing the right path. What are the different types of paths? There is path of Goodness, Passion and Ignorance. How does one choose the right path? By performing right actions.

There is a famous saying action speaks louder than words. Every action you take eventually becomes your habit and that transforms to becoming your nature. If you want to become a happy person or want a happy marriage or seek happiness at work, look at the actions you are doing every day. Ask yourself are my actions leading me to the path of happiness or sadness? Lets see what happens when you walk on these different paths.

There was a man who was a friend of my friend; he was killing himself each day by walking on the path of ignorance. He didn't want to work because he had money. He sold his shop and kept his money in fixed deposits. His daily routine was to wake up late, catch a friend to have breakfast out then skip lunch. Do nothing all day except to watch TV. Then sit alone or with a friend to have drinks till late and order food from a restaurant on a daily basis. His girlfriend left him looking at his behavior. His friends advised him to change his ways, but he didn't want to listen to anyone. His family gave up on him. He was just eating, sleeping and risking his health by eating outside food everyday and putting on weight. By walking on the path of ignorance and laziness, he found friends named sadness, loneliness and depression.

The character of Kabir Singh played by actor Shahid Kapoor in the movie "Kabir Singh" displayed a dark character where Kabir is shown as a very aggressive angry stubborn lover who took alcohol, sex and drugs while at work to deal with his deep depression of separation from the girl whom he loved like crazy. You can clearly see that this character too walked on the path of ignorance and madness.

Today with the kind of metro life we lead. From morning rushing to work then coming home late evenings, having dinner sleeping then again going to work next day. We some how have failed to connect with family and friends. Some think do we really have the time, money and energy to manage families coming over to stay or friends coming over to party. We think twice before spending money on family and friends or even on ourselves. We become conservative in our mindset because of this we avoid going out having get-together, we even avoid going to meet our extended or real family by giving them work load reasons of not having time to meet them up. We meet clients and customers over for dinner or lunch only on the motive of getting business in return. This kind of action speaks of our selfishness and greediness attitude when it comes to spending time or money. This becomes our habit, eventually people start maintaining distances and consider us to be a selfish person with lots of attitude. By walking on the path of passion we loose out on our real friends and family and befriend selfishness and greed.

The character played by actor Shahid Kapoor in the movie "Badmaash Company" displayed a character that is overcome by greed wherein he only thinks of ideas to make money by duping people. With that attitude he slowly looses out on his friends and family. This character too walked on the path of passion and greed.

Every time I happen to meet a happy married couple I always ask them the reason to their happy marriage, "Both of you must have faced problems in your relationship? How did you overcome it? I hear mostly couples constantly fight over petty issues. What is your secret of successful married life?" The answer was care and understanding. Wife said, "My husband always helped me in small little things like giving a helping hand in daily household chores. Simple help in the kitchen or with the groceries or cleaning of dishes or cooking has sprinkled the magic of goodness in our relationship, which kept us going in the right direction. Small acts of goodness always bought smiles whenever I felt angry, this action changed our life." By walking on the path of goodness, they found friends named respect, peace, happiness, care, love and trust.

The character played by actor Shahid Kapoor in the movie "Vivaah" displayed a strong emotional character that is full of goodness wherein he and his family accepts the girl whom he was about to get married to with full love and respect in spite knowing that she got severe burns during the marriage ceremony. This character purely walked on the path of goodness, respect and love.

In the Bhagavad Gita, on the battlefield of Kurukshetra, Lord Krishna explained to Arjuna about the three modes of material nature namely goodness, passion and ignorance. Lord mentioned that every living entity is controlled by these three modes. Lord Krishna clearly told Arjuna that, "The mode of goodness, being purer than the others, frees one from all sinful reactions. Those situated in that mode become influenced by a sense of happiness and knowledge."

"The mode of passion is born of unlimited desires and longings and because of this the living entity is bound to material fruitive actions."

"The mode of darkness, born of ignorance, is misleading all living entities. The results of this mode are madness, inactivity, laziness and sleep, which binds the conditioned soul."

You have the right to choose which path you want to walk on. Let the choice of walking on the path of goodness come from within. Promise yourself today that whatever action you take, shall be for the goodness to others and you will give your 100%. Always choose to walk on the path of goodness over passion and Ignorance. Commit yourself to walk on the path of goodness and you shall meet great friends on your journey. Here is an important life lesson.

**Lesson No: 29 Walk on the path of Goodness by being kind and humble to others and give your 100% in whatever work you do. Be ready to help others without any selfish thoughts. When you love someone, love with all your heart and not with any hidden expectation. Always choose to walk on the path of Goodness over Passion and Ignorance.

Shikha raised her hand and asked, "I always feel confused and fail to choose the right man to fall in love and get married. Can you throw some light on this?" Sure, why not. There is an interesting conversation between Lord Krishna and Arjuna which every man and woman must hear.

Respect for Women

One day Arjuna asked Lord Krishna, "My dearest friend, how do you handle your 16108 wives?" Arjuna further said, "It's so difficult for a normal house hold husband to handle his wife." Lord Krishna smiled and said, "Good question Arjuna."

Lord Krishna further said, "It's Respect. When I had freed those 16100 women who were captured by a demon named Narakasura. Nobody accepted them because they were all labeled as sex slaves. They all were about to commit suicide that is why I married all of them to restore their honor."

"You can win any woman's heart by genuinely giving her the love and respect she deserves. In return you will get an amazing companion, who will shower your life with lots of love and compassion. When a man's nature is in the mode of 'Goodness' he gives love and respect not only to his loved ones but also to every woman, every person he meets be it at work or outside. He talks politely and kindly be it a poor person or a rich person. He chooses to be calm in the most difficult situation."

"If you look at a woman with the eyes hungry for sex, expect only sexual pleasure or any benefit. In return she too can use you for her benefit. What you give is what you get in return. If today you see a woman as a commodity to be bought or sold, in no time she will change the rules and make the man a commodity to be bought or sold. When a man's nature is in the mode of 'Passion' he becomes too engrossed in fulfilling his unlimited desires. He is highly attracted to the opposite sex. He always wants to enjoy sense gratification. He becomes selfish, restless and greedy."

"If you constantly abuse a woman, disrespect her, behave with her rudely, hit her and even rape her. Be it in marriage or when the women are single or divorced. You do not deserve to be a man. That's why when a man's nature is in the mode of 'Ignorance'. He behaves like a mad person, acts foolishly and becomes selfish. He is far from being religious, most of the time sleeping, tired all the time, nervous, tensed, filled with anxiety and gets addicted to drugs and alcohol."

"Arjuna, be it a man or a woman every body behaves according to the modes of his/her nature. It's important for a man to understand his nature and shift it in the mode of 'Goodness'. This can happen with the help of self-knowledge. He should not let ignorance destroy him and passion tie him to this world. Under the protection of 'Goodness', he shall be rescued from the grasp of anger, passion, greed, laziness and ignorance. Goodness can only show the path leading to God. One needs to rise above the three modes of nature and develop true love and devotion for God."

Lord Krishna had mentioned the same details to Arjuna on the battlefield of Kurukshetra, in the Bhagavad Gita. Lord Krishna said, "When the human being is able to transcend these three modes associated with the body, he can become free from birth, death, old age and their distresses and can enjoy nectar even in this life." This teaches us another life lesson.

Lesson No: 30 With the help of self-knowledge understand your true nature and shift it in the mode of "Goodness". You can win a woman's heart by genuinely giving her love and respect. Goodness can show the path leading to God. Rise above the three modes of nature and develop true love and devotion for God.

It's now time for lunch. I'm sure you all must be very hungry by now. Time now is 1.30 pm and we all will gather again at 2.30 pm.

CHAPTER 15

Arjuna Learn To Detach Yourself

"Hope you all had a delicious and filling lunch?" I asked. Everyone nodded. "Lets continue the session.

It's time to write something very interesting on your note pad. I want you to write down all the actions that brings smile to you. Time is 3 minutes.

Okay times up. I request 3 participants to come forward and share their list with everyone." There were lots of interesting things that they shared like watching a funny movie, travelling, shopping, having a haircut, catching up with a friend for coffee or dinner, listening to songs, reading jokes and so on.

"This chapter talks about detachment and it's very important to learn to let go from what stops us from smiling.

There are 20 Shlokas in Chapter 15 of The Bhagavad Gita. I request each participant to read one shloka each that is translated in English." Everyone started reading one after the other.

The Yoga of The Supreme Person

The Supreme Personality of Godhead said: It is said that there is an imperishable banyan tree that has its roots upward and its branches down and whose leaves are the Vedic religious songs. One who knows this tree is the knower of the Vedas.

The branches of this tree extend downward and upward, nourished by the three modes of material nature. The slender shoots of the tree are the objects of the senses. This tree also has roots going down, and these are bound to the fruitive actions of human society.

The real form of this tree cannot be understood in this world. No one can understand where it ends, where it begins, or where its foundation is. But with determination one must cut down this strongly rooted tree with the weapon of detachment. Thereafter, one must seek that place from which, having gone, one never returns, and there surrender to that Supreme Personality of Godhead from whom everything began and from whom everything has extended since time immemorial.

Those who are free from false prestige, false belief and false association, who understands the eternal, who are done with material lust, who are freed from the dualities of happiness and sorrow, and who, not confused, know how to surrender unto the Supreme Person attain to that eternal kingdom.

That supreme abode of Mine is not illumined by the sun or moon, nor by fire or electricity. Those who reach it never return to this material world.

The living entities in this conditioned world are My eternal fragmental parts. Due to conditioned life, they are struggling very hard with the six senses, which include the mind.

The living entity in the material world carries his different conceptions of life from one body to another, as the air carries aromas. Thus he takes one kind of body and again quits it to take another.

The living entity, thus taking another gross body, obtains a certain type of ear, eye, tongue, nose and sense of touch, which are grouped about the mind. He thus enjoys a particular set of sense objects.

The foolish cannot understand how a living entity can quit his body, nor can they understand what sort of body he enjoys under the spell of the modes of nature. But one whose eyes are trained in knowledge can see all this.

The aspiring transcendentalists, who are situated in self-realization, can see all this clearly. But those whose minds are not developed and who are not situated in self-realization cannot see what is taking place, though they may try.

The splendor of the sun, which helps disappear the darkness of this whole world, comes from Me. And the splendor of the moon and the splendor of fire are also from Me.

I enter into each planet, and by My energy they stay in orbit. I become the moon and thereby supply the juice of life to all vegetables.

I am the fire of digestion in the bodies of all living entities, and I join with the air of life, outgoing and incoming, to digest the four kinds of foodstuff.

I am seated in everyone's heart, and from Me come remembrance, knowledge and forgetfulness. By all the Vedas, I am to be known. Indeed, I am the compiler of Vedanta, and I am the knower of the Vedas.

There are two classes of beings, the imperfect and the perfect. In the material world every entity is imperfect, and in the spiritual world every entity is called perfect.

Besides these two, there is the greatest living personality, the Supreme Soul, the imperishable Lord Himself, who has entered the three worlds and is maintaining them.

Because I am transcendental, beyond both the imperfect and the perfect, and because I am the greatest, I am celebrated both in the world and in the Vedas as that Supreme Person.

Whoever knows Me as the Supreme Personality of Godhead, without doubting, is the knower of everything. He therefore engages himself in full devotional service to Me, O son of Bharata.

This is the most confidential part of the Vedic scriptures, O sinless one, and it is disclosed now by Me. Whoever understands this will become wise, and his efforts will know perfection.

Let Me Now Summarize Chapter 15:

Here Lord Krishna talks about detachment. When one is able to detach himself from false prestige, false belief, false association, lust, happiness and sorrow. The one who is not confused, who understands Lord Krishna as the Supreme Personality of Godhead surrenders unto Him and engages in His devotional service attains to His eternal kingdom. Those who reach Lord's supreme abode never return to this material world. This is the most confidential part of the Vedic scriptures. Whoever understands this becomes wise.

I asked everyone, "Can anyone tell me what do you understand from this chapter?" One participant replied, "We must learn to detach ourselves to live peacefully." Another participant said, "Madam having the knowledge that one must remain detached is one thing, but can you tell us some practical examples of how to do it." I smiled and said, "Sure. Listen carefully.

Smile Your Way

Can you smile when you are angry? Can you smile when you are sad? Can you smile when you are depressed?

The answer is "Yes you can", only when you learn to detach yourself emotionally.

Let me share with you, how?

One day a man was doing his daily routine work. Suddenly people started insulting and abusing him. One person said, "You are an idiot", the other said, "You are good for nothing", the third person said, "You are a coward". The man listened silently, smiled and said, "If you have finished can I continue doing my work. If you have something more to say, you can continue after I finish with my work. People were surprised. They said, "What kind of a man are you. We are insulting you, abusing you, still you are not reacting and instead you are smiling". The man said, "I am my own master, you cannot force me to do something. I decide and choose to act. Without my reaction, your action has no meaning". People were shocked, they asked, "Who are you?" Do you want to know who that man really was? He was my grandfather. So smile, when you come across tough people on your way.

One day I happened to see some video on Facebook, where a man told that he recently lost his wife and he was feeling guilty of not being able to save her life and now those negative thoughts are troubling him every time. It reminded me of my personal story with my mother when she was on wheelchair. "Muma I got a job in Delhi, but I don't want to leave you and go". Muma said, "Go, don't worry about me I will be fine". After 1 month I got a bad news that she passed away. "Muma if I would have known that I'm going to loose you forever, I wouldn't have gone. I feel so guilty and hurt within myself that how could I leave you. If I had not gone, you would have been alive". We all love our dear ones and have great attachment. When our loved one dies, we become insane and blame ourselves. But, then I chose to accept and respect her departed soul, instead of blaming myself. So smile, whenever you think of your loved ones and remember the happy moments on your way.

Many years back, my very dear friend was in a relationship with a guy for 3 years. But, her boyfriend fell in love with someone else and chose to get married to the other girl in his life. My friend was deeply hurt by his rejection but could not do anything. Instead she started sleeping with other guys because she was frustrated. She used to feel guilty of her acts, but she also got addicted to having sex with multiple guys. This was only when I made her realize what she was doing was wrong, its better to forgive that guy by accepting and respecting his decision of choosing someone else as his life partner, only then did my friend become truly free and happy. She learnt the most important lesson of her life that if you love someone let him or her go. If that person truly loves you he or she will come back else we just need to accept this truth. So smile, whenever you face problems in your relationships and learn to let go on your way.

Now days whenever I get angry or I feel sad, I sit in front of the mirror and talk my heart out about my problem. This exercise helps me calm down and finally the person in the mirror says, "Sheetal don't worry everything will be fine. Just SMILE". There I smile and my anger just flies away. I have made a promise with myself, that I will always remember to smile whenever I feel sad, depressed and angry. So smile and win hearts of everyone on your way.

"Pain will leave you, when you learn to let go".

"Train yourself to let go of everything you fear to loose".

The nature of our mind is such that it gets attached to some object, place or person very badly. In such a state, our mind is swayed by the emotions than the intellect. We always think of that object, place or person and without it our life seems impossible. Too much attachment to anything is also called infatuation and it is the cause of most sorrows. We are always thinking of it and without that thing or person, our life seems impossible. Due to such infatuation our mind always wanders and forgets other important things in life. So smile and learn to let go any attachment on your way.

In the Bhagavad Gita, Lord Krishna teaches Arjuna to live in this world without getting attached to anything or any being. The being who has taken birth is sure to die and will take birth again. The body dies but not the soul. So detach and free yourself from the anger triggered by others, from sorrow caused by the death of our loved ones, let go the people whom we love so much, find new ideas to smile, win everyone's hearts, let go any attachments and always remember to smile on your way. Here are two important life lessons.

**Lesson No: 31 Detach and free yourself from anger and sorrow caused by others or any situation. Free yourself emotionally from people whom you love, learn to let go. Let go any attachments.

**Lesson No: 32 Always keep smiling, not only when you are happy but even when you feel sad, depressed, stressed and angry.

One participant raised his hand and asked, "What do you have to say about ego, how can we detach ourselves and overcome our biggest enemy ego." There is an interesting conversation that happens between few saints. Let's hear it.

Ego Vs. Love

Once a group of saints were discussing about their problems. One saint said, "It is getting so difficult for us to teach the modern man about Spirituality. He simply refuses to acknowledge wisdom coming from the ancient scriptures. He says, "I don't want to teach my children about Spirituality, it doesn't work in today's times." The other saint said, "Man is busy in making money, building assets knowing very well that he won't be taking any of these with him after death." Some other saint added, "He also complains that he is not happy nor having peace of mind." Another saint said, "He only wants name, fame and success to boost his ego."

The leader of all the saints was listening and said, "Can anyone tell me under what circumstances was Lord Krishna born?" One saint replied, "Oh yes, Lord Krishna was the eight's son born to mother Devaki and father Vasudeva. Devaki's brother was King Kansa. When King Kansa, was transporting his sister Devaki and her husband by chariot after their wedding, he heard an astral voice from the sky made a prophecy, telling him that her eighth child would kill him. His initial response was to kill Devaki outright, thus nullifying the chance that any of her children might slay him. But Vasudeva pleaded for her life, saying that he would deliver any child she bore into Kansa's hands. The demonic king agreed to this proposition but went one step further: he locked them in his prison, so there would be no possibility of them deceiving him and letting their children go free. King Kansa killed their six children one after the other. The seventh child got saved by miraculously transferring the unborn child from the womb of Devaki to the womb of Rohini. When the eighth child, Lord Krishna was born all the prison guards fell asleep, shackles broke and father Vasudeva could manage taking his newborn child Lord Krishna safely to his friend Nanda's house at Gokul by crossing river Yamuna. He then got his daughter who was just born in return as instructed by the Lord Himself. Upon hearing the news of the eight child, King Kansa came and took the child to smash her head to the wall. Immediately, the girl child took the divine form of Goddess Durga and laughed at King Kansa by saying, "The eighth son of Devaki is already born and He will kill you soon."

The leader of the saints said, "Very well. But do you know Lord Krishna's birth itself teaches a lot to us?"

He further said, "Mother Devaki and father Vasudeva represent the physical body. King Kansa represents Ego and Lord Krishna represents love. Ego cannot survive and has to bow down in front of love. That is why there is always a war between Ego and love, just like King Kansa and Lord Krishna. The prison guards represents our senses which is protecting our ego that keeps us engaged on the outside so that we cannot see the infinite source within. The Prison represents this material world. We too are trapped in this prison until we develop true love for God and only after Lord Krishna is born within us can we become free from this trap. Lord Krishna is the only One who can release us from our material sufferings and help us attain the freedom to return to His spiritual home."

The leader asked all the saints, "Have you ever seen a child?" All nodded with a big, "Yes". Then one saint asked, "What are you trying to explain to us?" The leader smiled and said, "A child has no worries whatsoever, he or she is happy and joyful all the time. A child represents God and to take rebirth as a child we need to let our ego die. When ego vanishes, your real birth happens. You receive true wisdom of self-knowledge."

He further said, "Even if the modern man doesn't wants to learn about spirituality out of ignorance, let's not get disturbed by this. We all must continue doing our duties by spreading the knowledge of self awareness, because unless he kills his ego he won't be able to experience true happiness and joy."

In the Bhagavad Gita, Lord Krishna told Arjuna that those who are free from ego, illusion and false association, who understands the eternal, who are free from lust, who are free from the dualities of happiness and sorrow, and those who are not confused, know how to surrender unto the Supreme Person, can attain to My eternal kingdom. Here is another important life lesson.

**Lesson No: 33 Ego cannot survive and has to bow down in front of love. Take rebirth by letting your ego die. Free yourself from the prison of suffering by experiencing the birth of Lord Krishna within you.

CHAPTER 16

Good People Bad People

"It's time to move to the next chapter. Here are the handouts, please pass it to everyone. This is a multiple-choice quiz for all of you to tick mark. It's a personality quiz and I will soon tell you why it's important. Now, this is a confidential quiz where only you will keep all answers to yourself and no one will be called in front to share their answers, so feel free to answer all of them. Time is 3 minutes.

Personality Quiz

Q1. How important is sex in your life?

A1. Very very important to such an extent that you cannot think of having a relationship with a female partner if she doesn't matches your sex drive.

A2. It's important to keep the relationship, marriage and family life going.

A3. Sex is important in a relationship irrespective of however your partner is, but you are willing to adjust and compromise on this part.

A4. Sex is least important for you as you place love and respect way above it.

Q2. How often do you get angry?

A1. Very often

A2. Frequently

A3. Occasionally

A4. Not at all

Q3. To what extent you feel very attached to the people, places or things close to you.

A1. To a great extent

A2. To a limited extent

A3. You are attached but know how to let go

A4. You are not attached at all

Q4. What is the importance of money in your life?

A1. Very very important for you money is everything

A2. Money is important to lead a luxurious life

A3. Money is good enough to lead a good happy and fulfilled life

A4. Money is not important at all

Q5. What kind of a person are you?

A1. Very egotistic

A2. Egoistic

A3. Balanced

A4. Never had an ego issue with anyone

Okay times up. How did you all find this quiz? Some said, "Ok". Some said, "good". Some said, "We all want to know the importance of this quiz."

"All the 5 questions mentioned in the handout will determine your weakness and strengths. If anyone of you has ticked the 1st option of any question directly tells you your weakness. If anyone of you has ticked the 2nd option of any question that tells you your weakness again. Most of the people fall in 2nd option. If anyone of you has ticked the 3rd option of any question that tells you your strengths. People who choose 3rd option are the wise category. If anyone of you has ticked the 4th option of any question that tells you your biggest strengths. Very few people choose the 4th option.

This chapter talks about our strengths and weaknesses, good and bad qualities in each one of us. Lets try to understand it further.

There are 24 Shlokas in Chapter 16 of The Bhagavad Gita. I request each participant to read one shloka each that is translated in English." Everyone started reading one after the other.

The Divine and Demoniac Natures

The Supreme Personality of Godhead said: Fearlessness, purification of one's existence; cultivation of spiritual knowledge; charity; self-control; performance of sacrifice; study of the Vedas; sternness; simplicity; nonviolence; truthfulness; freedom from anger; giving up of; calmness; strong dislike to faultfinding; compassion for all living entities; freedom from strong desire of material possessions; gentleness; modesty; steady determination; strength; forgiveness; courage; cleanliness; and freedom from jealously and from the passion for honor--these transcendental qualities, O son of Bharata, belong to godly men blessed with divine nature.

Pride, arrogance, egoism, anger, harshness and ignorance--these qualities belong to those of demoniac nature, O son of Pritha.

The transcendental qualities are helpful to liberation, whereas the demoniac qualities make for bondage. Do not worry, O son of Pandu, for you are born with the divine qualities.

O son of Pritha, in this world there are two kinds of created beings. One is called divine and the other demoniac. I have already explained to you at length the divine qualities. Now hear from Me of the demoniac.

Those who are demoniac do not know what is to be done and what is not to be done. Neither cleanliness nor proper behavior nor truth is found in them.

They say that this world is unreal, with no foundation, no God in control. They say it is produced of sex desire and has no cause other than lust.

Following such conclusions, the demoniac, who are lost to themselves and who have no intelligence, engage in unbeneficial, horrible works meant to destroy the world.

Taking shelter of unquenchable sex and absorbed in excess of pride and false prestige, the demoniac, thus misguided, are always sworn to unclean work, attracted by the impermanent.

They believe that to satisfy the senses is the prime necessity of human civilization. Thus until the end of life their anxiety is immeasurable. Bound by a network of hundreds of thousands of desires and absorbed in lust and anger, they secure money by illegal means for sense satisfaction.

The demoniac person thinks: "So much wealth do I have today, and I will gain more according to my schemes. So much is mine now, and it will increase in the future, more and more. He is my enemy, and I have killed him, and my other enemies will also be killed. I am the lord of everything. I am the enjoyer. I am perfect, powerful and happy. I am the richest man, surrounded by aristocratic relatives. There is none so powerful and happy as I am. I shall perform sacrifices, I shall give some charity, and thus I shall rejoice." In this way, such persons are mislead by ignorance.

Thus puzzled by various worries and bound by a network of false believes, they become too strongly attached to sense enjoyment and falls down into hell.

Self-satisfied and always disrespectful, mislead by wealth and false prestige, they sometimes proudly perform sacrifices in name only, without following any rules or regulations.

Confused by false ego, strength, pride, lust and anger, the demons become jealous of the Supreme Personality of Godhead, who is situated in their own bodies and in the bodies of others, and curse against the real religion.

Those who are jealous and mischievous, who are the lowest among men, I continuously cast into the ocean of material existence, into various demoniac species of life.

Attaining repeated birth amongst the species of demoniac life, O son of Kunti, such persons can never approach Me. Gradually they sink down to the most inferior type of existence.

There are three gates leading to this hell-lust, anger, and greed. Every sane man should give these up, for they lead to the degradation of the soul.

The man who has escaped these three gates of hell, O son of Kunti, performs acts beneficial to self-realization and thus gradually attains the supreme destination.

He who rejects scriptural instructions and acts according to his own idea attains neither perfection, nor happiness, nor the supreme destination.

One should therefore understand what is duty and what is not duty by the regulations of the scriptures. Knowing such rules and regulations, one should act so that he may gradually be elevated.

Let Me Now Summarize Chapter 16:

In this chapter, Lord Krishna explains that in this world there are two kinds of beings one is divine the other is demonic. Lord further explained the divine qualities and demoniac qualities. Lord Krishna says that those who possess demoniac qualities do not follow the regulations of scriptures, attain lower births leading them to further material bondage. They are always confused because of false ego, strength, pride, lust and anger. They are jealous of Me, who is also situated in their own bodies and in the bodies of others. Such demoniac persons can never attain to Lord Krishna. But those who possess divine qualities who follow rules and regulations as mentioned in the scriptures, gradually attain spiritual destination. Lord Krishna tells that every sane person must give up on lust, anger and greed that are the three gates to hell, and perform actions that will lead to self-realization.

I asked everyone, "Can anyone tell me what do you understand from this chapter?" One participant replied, "We must learn to overcome lust, anger and greed to progress spiritually." Another participant said, "There are two kinds of people in this world one is divine or good people and other is demonic or bad people." Another participant asked, "Madam can you tell us more about how to give up on lust, anger and greed." I smiled and said, "Sure. Listen carefully.

Five Robbers

Do you know the five robbers who rob us and never let us travel on the path of spiritual enlightenment? They are none other than Kaam (lust), Krodh (anger), Moh (attachment), Lobh (greed), Ahankar (false pride). Anything done under their control will rob a person of their common sense and in turn destroy the person.

Once a household man was walking back to his home from work. It was late evening. Suddenly he saw five men coming towards him. He started feeling uncomfortable and felt they are up to something. These five men stood in front of him and said, "We are robbers and we have come to rob you." The man got frighten and didn't understand what to do. One of the robbers said, "Don't worry we are different kind of robbers not the ones who rob money." The man got confused and asked, "Get off my way, I have nothing to give, I'm an ordinary household man." The robbers got closer and said, "We won't leave you unless you pass our test." The man looked around for help but couldn't find anybody. He became helpless and with a low voice asked, "What test?" One of the robbers said, "Each one of us will ask you for something that you already have and in return we will give you 10 times of what you give to each one of us. Are you clear?" The man had no option but to say yes. He further asked, "Will you let me go if I pass your test?" The robbers shook their heads with affirmation.

The first robber came forward and asked the man, "I want to rob you of your loyalty towards your wife. Which means if you agree to be sexually disloyal to your wife, I will give you 10 times more women and amazing sexual experiences which only the royal men have that privilege. I know you are one-woman kind of man. I just want you to become the man for many women." The man smiled as he was imagining the wonderful life he will have with many women. The man asked, "How can you assure me of this transaction and how is it even possible? I am just an ordinary man. I don't even have that much amount of money to have so many women. After all women run behind wealthy men." The first robber smiled and said, "You will get both money and women. I'm not joking this all will be true. We are spirits from the unknown and have special powers." The man thought about it for sometime and said, "No I'm not interested, I'm very happy and satisfied with my wife. I love her a lot." After hearing this, the first robber disappeared.

The second robber came forward and asked the man, "I want to rob you of your calm and peace. Which means if you accept to give up your calmness and peacefulness, I will give you 10 times more power, strength and anger. This will make you a strong and powerful man, people will get scared of you and all your work will be done in no time. The man thought about it for sometime and said, "No I'm not interested, I'm very happy being calm and peaceful. I know anger leads to nowhere. The work gets done out of fear but with anger my entire well-being and health will get affected. Nobody loves an angry person." After hearing this, the second robber disappeared.

The third robber came forward and asked the man, "I want to rob you of your nature of detachment. Which means if you accept to give up your detachment, I will give you 10 times more attachment to worldly things you love like your house, your job or things like food, liquor, etc.. and even people whom you love like your wife, parents and friends. This will make you obsessive about things and people, even if you want to get rid of it you won't be able to. The man thought about it for sometime and said, "No

I'm not interested, I'm very happy being detached. I know attachment is not good. My mind will always be occupied of the things and people I am attached to. I will become a slave to my own attachments. I will always keep worrying about them." After hearing this, the third robber disappeared.

The fourth robber came forward and asked the man, "I want to rob you of your satisfaction in whatever you earn. Which means if you accept to give up your satisfaction from money, I will give you 10 times more money, gold, diamonds to buy anything you want like car, house, clothes, etc. This will make you greedy and aggressive for more. The man thought about it for sometime and said, "No I'm not interested, I'm very much satisfied with what I earn. Greed for anything is not good. My mind will always be occupied of how and where to invest, where to spend, more money means more headaches. I will always keep worrying about money." After hearing this, the fourth robber disappeared.

The fifth robber came forward and asked the man, "I want to rob you of your self confidence. Which means if you accept to give up your self-confidence, I will give you 10 times more false pride, ego, arrogance, etc. This will make you feel extremely proud, stubborn and you can get people to do exactly what you say. The man thought about it for sometime and said, "No I'm not interested, I'm very much satisfied being a humble and confident person. I myself do not like egotistic people. They act too pricy and do not treat people properly who are lower to them." After hearing this, the fifth robber before disappearing told the man, "You are a man who is truly devotional to God." The fifth robber disappeared.

The man sighed a relief after all of them disappeared. He thought to him, "Had I accepted anybody's offer, I surely would have destroyed my own life with my own hands. By thanking God, he went home and lived happily there after.

In Delhi there was a family of three-father, mother and a young son. The father was a well-known reputed Businessman who was running his chemical company very successfully. But, unfortunately his son got addicted to drugs. He was son of a rich father so he had all the money to buy drugs. Slowly as years passed by he started falling short of money, so he started drugging his own father and on his name and in the name of his father's company he borrowed money from lenders. He also extracted gold from his mother. He even drugged his own father because of which the father was always sleeping and in no time they had to sell their properties to pay to the lenders and they all came on street. The boy ran away from

· home and both his parents got separated. Then one day, this boy's friend who was also a drug addict died and he realized this is a signal to him from God. The boy decided he wanted to change and then met his uncle and he agreed to go to a de-addiction center. There the boy met with a doctor whose first objective was to make the patient understand and accept that he is addicted to drugs and he willingly really wants to come out of this problem with much needed help. There is a saying, "God helps those who help themselves." After the required counseling, finally when the boy was ready, his doctor just helped him come out of this addiction by focusing his attention on his hobbies, fitness, health, good food, books and by correcting his mindset. After few months, this boy got a new life and is now working in a reputed company. His parents too realized their mistakes of not keeping an eye on their son, which made them lose everything. So, take total charge and control of your life and with your will power and determination you will be able to fight with any robber that comes your way.

In the Bhagavad Gita, Lord Krishna tells Arjuna that there are three gates leading to hell-lust, anger, and greed. Every sane man should close these gates for they lead to the degradation of the soul. One should use his mind and common sense, realize his mistake, use his will power and determination and fight against these five robbers who are waiting to rob us and take us away from God. This brings us to another important life lesson.

Lesson No: 34 Take total charge and control of your life and fight against the five robbers Kaam (lust), Krodh (anger), Moh (attachment), Lobh (greed), Ahankar (false pride) using your mind, common sense, will power and determination.

One participant raised his hand and asked, "I do not know if I should say this, something just striked me. As its mentioned in The Bhagavad Gita that there are two types of people in this world good and divine, bad and demonic. Today the entire world is fighting with terrorism, what do you have to say on this? Is there a solution to this problem?" I smiled and said, "Honestly time will decide the solution, but there is an interesting story which I want to share it with all of you."

Game Changing Buffet Dinner

Recently representatives from across the world had gathered together to work out a solution to a major threat that the entire world is facing today,

"Terrorism". Everyone said, "We need freedom from fear, freedom from terrorists, freedom from threats, freedom from insecurity. We need to come together as one world and fight with the other demonic destructive world."

Lord Krishna was listening to all this and thought of taking a lead to sort this problem out once and for all.

One representative said, "Lets elect one person who is neutral, neither from any political country or background. One who understands both the world. Let's call Him a leader of humanity. A leader who will guide us in the right direction whom everyone will agree to, listen to and follow." Everyone agreed and one name was chosen and He was called to become leader of humanity. This person was none other than Lord Krishna disguised in human form.

Lord Krishna said, "Let's give this other demonic destructive world one chance to surrender and change their actions or else we will have no choice but to get together to have a war against terrorism. Just like how Lord Krishna had made several attempts to avoid the Mahabharata war between Kauravas and Pandavas. But He knew it was coming."

One Representative said, "But how do we do that?"

Lord Krishna said, "Let's invite the other demonic destructive world for dinner at a secret place. I will organize a big banquet. As they don't know Me they will surely come. At the end of the banquet we all will get our answers."

And Lord Krishna sent out invitations to the other demonic destructive world. On the appointed day, a most lavish banquet was organized and hundreds of terrorists arrived at that place.

The terrorists were an impatient lot, disorganized and noisy. They asked the host that they wanted VIP (very important person) treatment, and therefore wanted to have their food served fast.

The host agreed to their request on one condition that the terrorists would tie wooden planks to both hands when eating. The terrorists said that they had no objection to tying the wooden planks on both their hands when eating, provided they are served with delicious food.

All the terrorists had wooden planks tied to both their hands and they immediately sat on the long dinner table, seated one next to the other in one straight line. They were all very eager to be served with delicious food.

The first course of food arrived. It was the best smelling soup in a bowel with spoon. Now when the terrorists got spoons filled with the soup, they realized that they could not bend their hands to bring the spoons to their mouths. They tried to lift their hands over their heads and tilt the spoons with their mouths wide open. They got the soup falling in their eyes and all over the face and also on their expensive garments.

The terrorists got noisier, became angry and started swearing at the host. Some of the terrorists wanted to shoot the host. Some tried to restrain the other terrorists and they started fighting among themselves. The terrorists agreed that it was totally useless for them to remain at this banquet, as it was not possible to eat the food without bending their hands. It was impossible to eat the food without messing up their beautiful and expensive garments.

With angry words the terrorists were about to leave the banquet, when Lord Krishna said, "Wait for every problem there is a solution. Even when your hands are tied to the wooden planks, you still can relish the delicious food." One terrorist asked, "How is it possible?" Lord Krishna smiled and said, "With wooden planks tied to your hands, you cannot serve or eat yourself but you extend your hand to the person sitting next to you and then serve him. This way you can help each other and relish this delicious food." All terrorists thought about it, some liked the idea and agreed, but most of them disagreed on this arrangement and wanted to eat with their own hands and not help others. Some said, "This is no way to treat your guests by putting conditions, doing things your way without thinking about our pains and making our life miserable. They all started fighting amongst themselves and created a nuisance. Lord Krishna said, "Wait, this is exactly what you all are doing. By becoming a terrorist and killing innocent people in the name of God, you are also treating the lives of all innocent people without any value. You are doing things the way your leaders want you to do without thinking about the pains and sufferings the innocent people go through after your attacks. Have you ever thought what kind of a life they live by loosing their family members or by suffering on wheel chair for the rest of their life or by loosing their hands or legs or eyes by your explosions. What if any of your family member or loved one gets killed in these attacks. Will you be happy? Just by accepting to hold the gun in your hand and agree to become a terrorist you have become a demon and not God. Just think about it, will God be really happy seeing you do all this in His name? Has God come in front of you and commanded you to do all this? No, it's the demonic destructive people who have manipulated your mind into the wrong path and compelled you to choose this life."

One terrorist said, "What can we do now? If we agree to choose the right path and leave our life of being a terrorist, our leaders will kill us. Please guide us." Lord Krishna said, "Become fearless. The world is afraid of you because you have been trained to kill them. You are afraid of your leader because they have no problem in killing you. It's better to get together as a team and fight against your leader and free not only yourself but all your friends by helping them get out of this terrible mess or get killed so that at least you save yourself from killing innocent people."

"Just like the wooden planks tied to your hands, you cannot even serve yourself a proper meal similarly by having a gun in your hand and being labeled as a terrorist you cannot alone help yourself but you can help and guide your friends to choose the right path and together achieve the impossible."

All representatives had disguised themselves and were stunned to hear these insights from the leader of humanity. Further they were surprised to see what happened next. All terrorists spoke with each other and concluded to help each other not only by serving each other with delicious food but by also trying to help each other get out of this mess as a team. Some terrorists were adamant and left in anger.

Everyone was observing all that happened. Lord Krishna said, "The major difference between the good divine people and the destructive demonic people was the difference in their attitude of 'Giving' and the attitude of 'Taking.' The destructive demonic people were made to think only about their individual self-interest whereas the good divine people always thought about selflessly serving others. When you open your heart and help selflessly, you receive also much more than you give."

"If you have the attitude of **TAKING** you are possessed with selfish demands and desires. Therefore there is constant struggle, stress and strain leading to crimes, robbery, rapes, corruption, terrorism, selfish behavior which is becoming a threat to nation, community, family and individuals."

"The moment you change your attitude to **GIVING** by not becoming selfish automatically demands and desires drop. You will begin to experience harmony, peace and happiness. Life is to give, not to take. True happiness comes by serving one and all. Serve the nation; serve the society, the family and yourself. These are the elements of right living. We need to do service to maintain our proper spiritual well being. When we understand that our pleasures and pains are identical with those of our fellow beings. This is true love. The feeling of true love arises from purity. Such purity of love upgrades us to greater spiritual heights."

In the Bhagavad Gita, Lord Krishna said, "There are only two types of people in this world, the one possessing a divine nature and the other possessing a demoniac nature. Men possessing a demoniac nature do not know what is to be done and what is not to be done. Hence they possess neither purity (external or internal) nor good conduct nor even truthfulness." Here comes another life lesson.

**Lesson No: 35 Change your attitude to that of Giving and you will experience harmony, peace and happiness. True happiness comes by selflessly serving others. If you have the attitude of Taking, drop it now.

Now it's time for a short tea break. Time is 4 pm and we all will gather again at 4.20 pm.

CHAPTER 17

Arjuna Every Person Nature Is Different

"Welcome back from the tea break. Hope you all are feeling refreshed. We are now going to watch the trailer of 2 movies back to back, the movies are "Munna Bhai MBBS and Lage Raho Munnabhai". I'm sure all of you must have watched these two all time favorite Bollywood movies." Everyone nodded. "We will come back to the Munnabhai later as the Chapter proceeds.

There are 28 Shlokas in Chapter 17 of The Bhagavad Gita. I request each participant to read one shloka each that is translated in English." Everyone started reading one after the other.

The Divisions Of Faith

Arjuna inquired: O Krishna, what is the situation of those who do not follow the principles of scripture but worship according to their own imagination? Are they in goodness, in passion or in ignorance?

The Supreme Personality of Godhead said: According to the modes of nature acquired by the embodied soul, one's faith can be of three kinds—in goodness, in passion or in ignorance. Now hear about this.

O son of Bharata, according to one's existence under the various modes of nature, one evolves a particular kind of faith. The living being is said to be of a particular faith according to the modes he has acquired.

Men in the mode of goodness worship the demigods; those in the mode of passion worship the demons; and those in the mode of ignorance worship ghosts and spirits.

Those who undergo severe severity and self-punishment not recommended in the scriptures, performing them out of pride and egoism, who are driven by lust and attachment, who are foolish and who torture the material elements of the body as well as the Supersoul dwelling within, are to be known as demons.

Even the food each person prefers is of three kinds, according to the three modes of material nature. The same is true of sacrifices, severities and charity. Now hear of the distinctions between them.

Foods dear to those in the mode of goodness increase the duration of life, purify one's existence and give strength, health, happiness and satisfaction. Such foods are juicy, fatty, wholesome and pleasing to the heart.

Foods that are too bitter, too sour, salty, hot, strong taste, dry and burning are dear to those in the mode of passion. Such foods cause distress, misery and disease.

Food prepared more than three hours before being eaten, food that is tasteless, spoilt and rotten, and food consisting of leftover and untouchable things is dear to those in the mode of darkness.

Of sacrifices, the sacrifice performed according to the directions of scripture, as a matter of duty, by those who desire no reward, is of the nature of goodness.

But the sacrifice performed for some material benefit, or for the sake of pride, O chief of the Bharatas, you should know to be in the mode of passion.

Any sacrifice performed without regard for the directions of scripture, without distribution of prasadam [spiritual food], without chanting of Vedic religious songs and payment to the priests, and without faith is considered to be in the mode of ignorance.

Severity of the body consists in worship of the Supreme Lord, the brahmanas, the spiritual master, and superiors like the father and mother, and in cleanliness, simplicity, celibacy and nonviolence.

Severity of speech consists in speaking words that are truthful, pleasing, beneficial, and not disturbing to others, and also in regularly reciting Vedic literature.

And satisfaction, simplicity, gravity, self-control and purification of one's existence are the severities of the mind.

This threefold severity, performed with transcendental faith by men not expecting material benefits but engaged only for the sake of the Supreme, is called severity in goodness.

Self-punishment performed out of pride and for the sake of gaining respect, honor and worship is said to be in the mode of passion. It is neither stable nor permanent.

Self-punishment performed out of foolishness, with self-torture or to destroy or injure others is said to be in the mode of ignorance.

Charity given out of duty, without expectation of return, at the proper time and place, and to a worthy person is considered to be in the mode of goodness.

But charity performed with the expectation of some return, or with a desire for fruitive results, or in half-hearted mood, is said to be charity in the mode of passion.

And charity performed at an impure place, at an improper time, to unworthy persons, or without proper attention and respect is said to be in the mode of ignorance.

From the beginning of creation, the three words om tat sat were used to indicate the Supreme Absolute Truth. These three symbolic representations were used by brahmanas while chanting the religious songs of the Vedas and during sacrifices for the satisfaction of the Supreme.

Therefore, transcendentalists undertake performances of sacrifice, charity and self-punishment in accordance with scriptural regulations begin always with 'om', to attain the Supreme.

Without desiring fruitive results, one should perform various kinds of sacrifice, self-punishment and charity with the word 'tat'. The purpose of such transcendental activities is to get free from the material entanglement.

The Absolute Truth is the objective of devotional sacrifice, and it is indicated by the word 'sat'. The performer of such sacrifice is also called 'sat', as are all works of sacrifice, self-punishment and charity which, true to the absolute nature, are performed to please the Supreme Person, O son of Pritha.

Anything done as sacrifice, charity or self-punishment without faith in the Supreme, O son of Pritha, is impermanent. It is called 'asat' and is useless both in this life and the next.

Let Me Now Summarize Chapter 17:

One's faith is of three types, in goodness, in passion and in ignorance, which evolve from the three modes of material nature. Men in mode of goodness worship demigods, in mode of passion worship demons and in mode of ignorance worship ghosts and spirits. Even foods that we eat are of three kinds according to the mode of nature. Also sacrifice, severity, self-punishment and charity are of three kinds according to the mode of nature. Action performed by those people whose faith is in passion and ignorance gain only materialistic results, whereas action performed in goodness, in accordance with scriptural instructions lead to pure faith in Lord Krishna.

I asked everyone, "Can anyone tell me what do you understand from this chapter?" One participant replied, "Everything we do, think, believe are of three types goodness, passion and ignorance." Another participant asked, "Madam can you tell us something more about belief. How can we believe in something or someone? I said, "Sure.

What You Believe Is What You Achieve

A man asked someone, "Do you believe in God?" The other person said, "Yes". He said, "But I can't see God, then how can I believe in Him? Seeing is believing right?" We all have a certain belief system based on our experiences and teachings. If a poor man believes that he can never get rich and that he is destined to be this way, he never attempts to even dream of becoming rich. The base of all our dreams, aspirations, a person whom we look up to, our thought process is based on our beliefs.

Around 15 years back I was very keen to do something of my own, start some business. After doing a lot of introspection I realized I love training people and want to make a career in same field. I was lucky enough to find a mentor who was a very senior retired trainer and a known family friend, with whom I got into partnership and started my entrepreneurial journey. But I didn't start with training, as my mentor told me that it requires a lot of experience and grey hair. So I started my journey as recruitment consultant. Unfortunately, after 3 years into business, my partner and mentor expired and I continued the business of recruitments. For so many years I believed I am not experienced enough to do training and didn't even think of shifting business or pursing it as another career option. Only while writing this book I realized I can guide, train and help people by solving their personal and professional problems through The Bhagavad Gita by giving speeches and conducting workshops as Life coach also I can guide job seekers on how they can find their dream job by conducting workshops and sharing my vast experience of 14 years into recruitments. So when you believe in yourself you start walking on the path of goodness. If you believe in yourself you can achieve your true potential.

My cousin from Delhi was a great follower of a famous Godman. He used to like his talks and teachings. Obviously because of his great talks and public speaking skills he managed to have so many followers. But I used to always wonder why do people treat a human being as God. It is nice to become a follower of a saint and implement the great teachings and learning in our life. But the fact is that he is just a human being and we give him designation similar to that of God. A time came when that Godman was convicted for rape. Can God ever rape a woman? Can God kill innocent followers? No. In today's world saints who call themselves to be God in human form are just doing business to con people. People who believe in them have their faith moving on the path of passion. If you believe in Godmen you achieve nothing.

Recently I read in a leading newspaper that now couples who got married from different religion or faiths have decided to raise their children religion free. Now days it's a trend to get married to someone who is from a different religion or faith if someone has fallen in love. In earlier times society used to object for a reason. In today's times it has been seen that in many families there is a constant struggle for both the husband and wife to adjust with their respective in-laws as well as society when it comes to deciding things relating to religious activities. The wife or mother wants to raise her children based on her religion or faith and the husband or father or the in-laws want the children to be raised as per their religion or faith. Ultimately the couples who do not want to accept their spouse's religion or faith and those who have decided to stick to their respective individuality are now raising their children without any values or religion. How good is that? From being born in a certain religion to choosing to get married to someone out of one's own religion and faith to raising children without any strong foundation is a faith moving on the path of ignorance. If you believe in no religion you achieve a dark future.

In the Bhagavad Gita, Lord Krishna explained to Arjuna about faith, which is of three kinds goodness, passion, or ignorance that is according to the modes of nature acquired by the embodied soul. Having belief in ourselves helps us achieve our true potential, our belief can make a human equal to God and our belief can erase religion all together. When someone believes in doing good work for society, people oppose him, criticize him but in the end the only thing that makes him win is the belief he carries within himself. Here comes another life lesson.

Lesson No: 36 Believe in yourself, you will achieve your true potential this will keep you moving on the right path.

One participant raised his hand and asked, "Madam today every one has some problem or the other, what do you think is the root cause of all problems and what is the solution to it?" Another participant said, "We all are keen to know how Munnabhai is linked with this chapter." I smiled and said, "Here comes an interesting story that I want to share it with all of you.

Difficult People

One day two friends were sitting near the sea watching the sunrise. Both of them are best of friends, one is emotionally sensitive and physically strong person and the other is practical, strong but foolish. Let's call the first one Munna bhai and the second one Circuit.

Munna said to Circuit, "Do you know I got a dream last night in that Lord Krishna appeared and asked me for a wish." Circuit asked, "So bhai what did you wish for?" Munna smiled and said, "I asked Lord Krishna, my brothers and sisters are very upset in their lives they are fighting with their problems everyday, give me magical powers to help them." Circuit asked, "Then what happened bhai." Munna said, "God smiled, blessed me and disappeared." Circuit asked, "Bhai then what happened?" Munna said, "Suddenly this golden book appeared like magic in my hands." Circuit enquired, "Bhai what happened when you opened the book?"

Munna said, "When I opened the book on the first page it read, 'This book will answer all your questions to achieve happiness and peace in everyone's life.' Then I turned the page to read what's next it read, 'Ask your problem and this book will give you the solution.' I immediately asked, 'What is the root cause of stress in today's world?' As I spoke, my words were getting typed on the book like magic. Then I turned to the next page and the answer came, 'Not knowing how to handle difficult people.' I asked, 'How does one manage people?' Immediately the solution appeared on the next page like some unseen divine energy was writing the answer. It read:

1. Try to understand the nature of the person you are dealing with.

2. Observe his/her behavior towards other people.

3. Enquire about the thoughts he/she carries towards the Supreme Lord.

4. Ask them about the kind of food they like to eat.

5. The kind of sacrifice they have done or believe in.

6. What do they think about certain things or situations?

7. What are the kinds of words they use while speaking or how do they speak.

8. Discuss with them about how they do charity.

The page then turned automatically and it read.

'If the person behaves nicely, treats people well, thinks about helping others, believes in praying to God, eats good balanced healthy fresh food on time, he sacrifices his happiness and achievements for others, thinks positive in every situation, speaks truth and doesn't hurt anyone, believes in giving charity out of love and concern is said to be in Goodness. Such a person is loved by all.'

'If a person shows lots of attitude, treats people nicely only if he wants something from them in return, thinks only about himself, believes in praying to humans who portray to be Gods, eats food that are either too hot, too sour or too salty unhealthy at irregular time even skips meals leaving his own body food deprived, he is ready to sacrifice only if he sees some benefit for himself, thinks positive and negative both in all situations, speaks diplomatically with everyone, gives charity but will make sure his name is recognized is said to be in Passion. Such a person only wants to be successful at any cost.'

'If a person behaves rudely, treats people abusively, think only about hurting others, does not believe in God, eats food that is stale leftover, he does sacrifice which is not according to scriptures and do not follow rules and regulations, thinks only negative in all situations, speaks words that hurt, gives charity to unworthy persons without any respect is said to be in Ignorance. Such a person has a negative mindset.'

Pages turned and the book revealed further answers.

'So once you understand the nature of the person you need to decide how you want to deal with him/her.'

'It is very easy and peaceful to deal with people who are good. People who are of the nature of passion can be dealt by a give and take strategy. People who are ignorant by nature, it is very difficult to deal with them as they will not listen or follow a positive path. Best strategy is to stay away from such people who are abusive verbally and physically. Be silent when you are with people who think and talk negative. It's important to seek professional help or personal advise from friends and family to deal with difficult situations caused by difficult people.'

Next page, For example:

'If a person is disturbed by a negative partner who is nagging all the time bringing stress and anxiety, who refuses to compromise or save his/her marriage its best to seek divorce. Seeking divorce is a sign of goodness and nagging is a sign of ignorance.'

'If an employee remains stressed at work not due to work pressure but due to his/her boss, it's time you look for better options is a sign of goodness.'

'If two women say mother-in-law and daughter-in-law are having fights its better to compromise and one learns to remain silent during arguments for the sake of the entire family and live together peacefully is a sign of goodness, else staying separately is another alternative but it is a sign of passion.'

'When a client shouts at you for work not delivered properly or on time or your subordinate makes a mistake, accepting it by apologizing and assuring to deliver by committing is a sign of goodness.'

'When a husband and wife fight with each other and one of them apologizes to maintain peace is a sign of goodness.'

'When there is a give and take in a marriage means dowry is a sign of passion.'

'When a person wants to achieve success in work or business and compromises on his principles is a sign of passion.'

Circuit said to Munna, "Wow bhai now you can help everyone."

Munna smiled and said, "That I can but every person must recognize his nature and try to consciously change it to goodness and develop faith in Lord Krishna by becoming his devotee."

In the Bhagavad Gita, Lord Krishna explained Arjuna about the different kinds of people distinguished based on their faith with respect to worship, then the kind of food they eat, the sacrifices they do, the severity of body, speech and mind they follow, the self-punishment and the kind of charity they do. The reason was to enlighten Arjuna about the differences between Pandavas and Kauravas so as to encourage him to fight for his rights, which has been wrongly possessed by Duryodhana. This brings us to yet another life lesson.

Lesson No: 37 Every person must recognize his nature and try to consciously change it to goodness and develop faith in Lord Krishna by becoming His devotee. People who are of the nature of passion can be dealt by a give and take strategy. People who are ignorant by nature, it is best to stay away from such people who are abusive verbally and physically. Be silent when you are with people who think and talk negative.

CHAPTER 18

Arjuna Let Go Your Self Doubt

"We have now come to the end of the session.

There are 78 Shlokas in Chapter 18 of The Bhagavad Gita. I request each participant to read two shlokas each that is translated in English." Everyone started reading one after the other.

Conclusion-The Perfection of Renunciation

Arjuna said: O mighty-armed one, I wish to understand the purpose of renunciation [tyaga] and of the renounced order of life [sannyasa], O killer of the Keshi demon, master of the senses.

The Supreme Personality of Godhead said: The giving up of activities that are based on material desire is what great learned men call the renounced order of life [sannyasa]. And giving up the results of all activities is what the wise call renunciation [tyaga].

Some learned men declare that all kinds of fruitive activities should be given up as faulty, yet other sages maintain that acts of sacrifice, charity and self-punishment should never be left.

O best of the Bharatas, now hear My judgment about renunciation. O tiger among men, renunciation is declared in the scriptures to be of three kinds.

Acts of sacrifice, charity and self-punishment are not to be given up; they must be performed. Indeed, sacrifice, charity and self-punishment purify even the great souls.

All these activities should be performed without attachment or any expectation of result. They should be performed as a matter of duty, O son of Pritha. That is My final opinion.

Prescribed duties should never be renounced. If one gives up his prescribed duties because of false belief, such renunciation is said to be in the mode of ignorance.

Anyone who gives up prescribed duties as troublesome or out of fear of bodily discomfort is said to have renounced in the mode of passion. Such action never leads to the elevation of renunciation.

O Arjuna, when one performs his prescribed duty only because it ought to be done, and renounces all material association and all attachment to the fruit, his renunciation is said to be in the mode of goodness.

The intelligent renouncer situated in the mode of goodness, neither hateful of inauspicious work nor attached to auspicious work, has no doubts about work.

It is indeed impossible for an embodied being to give up all activities. But he who renounces the fruit of action is called one who has truly renounced.

For one who is not renounced, the threefold fruits of action--desirable, undesirable and mixed--follow after death. But those who are in the renounced order of life have no such results to suffer or enjoy.

O mighty-armed Arjuna, according to the Vedanta there are five causes for the accomplishment of all action. Now learn of these from Me.

The place of action [the body], the performer, the various senses, the many different kinds of attempts, and ultimately the Supersoul— these are the five factors of action.

Whatever right or wrong action a man performs by body, mind or speech is caused by these five factors.

Therefore one who thinks himself the only doer, not considering the five factors, is certainly not very intelligent and cannot see things as they are.

One who is not motivated by false ego, whose intelligence is not trapped, though he kills men in this world, does not kill. Nor is he bound by his actions.

Knowledge, the object of knowledge, and the knower are the three factors that motivate action; the senses, the work and the doer are the three constituents of action.

According to the three different modes of material nature, there are three kinds of knowledge, action, and performer of action. Now hear of them from Me.

That knowledge by which one undivided spiritual nature is seen in all living entities, though they are divided into innumerable forms, you should understand to be in the mode of goodness.

That knowledge by which one sees that in every different body there is a different type of living entity you should understand to be in the mode of passion.

And that knowledge by which one is attached to one kind of work as the all in all, without knowledge of the truth, and which is very limited, is said to be in the mode of darkness.

That action which is regulated and which is performed without attachment, without love or hatred, and without desire for fruitive results is said to be in the mode of goodness.

But action performed with great effort by one seeking to satisfy his desires, and enacted from a sense of false ego, is called action in the mode of passion.

That action performed in false belief, in disregard of scriptural instructions, and without concern for future bondage or for violence or pain caused to others is said to be in the mode of ignorance.

One who performs his duty without association with the modes of material nature, without false ego, with great determination and enthusiasm, and without wavering in success or failure is said to be a worker in the mode of goodness.

The worker who is attached to work and the fruits of work, desiring to enjoy those fruits, and who is greedy, always jealous, impure, and moved by joy and sorrow, is said to be in the mode of passion.

The worker who is always engaged in work against the instructions of the scripture, who is materialistic, stubborn, cheating and expert in insulting others, and who is lazy, always bad-tempered and postponing actions is said to be a worker in the mode of ignorance.

O winner of wealth, now please listen as I tell you in detail of the different kinds of understanding and determination, according to the three modes of material nature.

O son of Pritha, that understanding by which one knows what ought to be done and what ought not to be done, what is to be feared and what is not to be feared, what is binding and what is liberating, is in the mode of goodness.

O son of Pritha, that understanding which cannot distinguish between religion and irreligion, between action that should be done and action that should not be done, is in the mode of passion.

That understanding which considers irreligion to be religion and religion to be irreligion, under the spell of false belief and darkness, and strives always in the wrong direction, O Partha, is in the mode of ignorance.

O son of Pritha, that determination which is unbreakable, which is sustained with firm and unwavering by yoga practice, and which thus controls the activities of the mind, life and senses is determination in the mode of goodness.

But that determination by which one holds fast to fruitive results in religion, economic development and sense satisfaction is of the nature of passion, O Arjuna.

And that determination which cannot go beyond dreaming, fearfulness, sorrow, depression and false belief--such unintelligent determination, O son of Pritha, is in the mode of darkness.

O best of the Bharatas, now please hear from Me about the three kinds of happiness by which the conditioned soul enjoys, and by which he sometimes comes to the end of all distress.

That which in the beginning may be just like poison but at the end is just like nectar and which awakens one to self-realization is said to be happiness in the mode of goodness.

That happiness which is derived from contact of the senses with their objects and which appears like nectar at first but poison at the end is said to be of the nature of passion.

And that happiness which is blind to self-realization, which is misleading from beginning to end and which arises from sleep, laziness and false belief is said to be of the nature of ignorance.

There is no being existing, either here or among the demigods in the higher planetary systems, which is freed from these three modes born of material nature.

Brahmanas, kshatriyas, vaishyas and shudras are distinguished by the qualities born of their own natures in accordance with the material modes, O chastiser of the enemy.

Peacefulness, self-control, severity, purity, tolerance, honesty, knowledge, wisdom and religiousness--these are the natural qualities by which the brahmanas work.

Heroism, power, determination, resourcefulness, courage in battle, generosity, and leadership are the natural qualities of work for the kshatriyas.

Farming, cow protection and business are the natural work for the vaishyas, and for the shudras there is labor and service to others.

By following his qualities of work, every man can become perfect. Now please hear from Me how this can be done.

By worship of the Lord, who is the source of all beings and who is present everywhere, a man can attain perfection through performing his own work.

It is better to engage in one's own occupation, even though one may perform it imperfectly, than to accept another's occupation and perform it perfectly. Duties prescribed according to one's nature are never affected by sinful reactions.

Every effort is covered by some fault, just as fire is covered by smoke. Therefore one should not give up the work born of his nature, O son of Kunti, even if such work is full of fault.

One who is self-controlled and unattached and who disregards all material enjoyments can obtain, by practice of renunciation, the highest perfect stage of freedom from reaction.

O son of Kunti, learn from Me how one who has achieved this perfection can attain to the supreme perfectional stage, Brahman, the stage of highest knowledge, by acting in the way I shall now summarize.

Being purified by his intelligence and controlling the mind with determination, giving up the objects of sense satisfaction, being freed from attachment and hatred, one who lives in a undisturbed place, who eats little, who controls his body, mind and power of speech, who is always in hypnotic state and who is detached, free from false ego, false strength, false pride, lust, anger, and acceptance of material things, free from false proprietorship, and peaceful--such a person is certainly elevated to the position of self-realization.

One who is thus transcendentally situated at once realizes the Supreme Brahman and becomes fully joyful. He never complaints or desires to have anything. He is equally inclined towards every living entity. In that state he attains pure devotional service unto Me.

One can understand Me as I am, as the Supreme Personality of Godhead, only by devotional service. And when one is in full consciousness of Me by such devotion, he can enter into the kingdom of God.

Though engaged in all kinds of activities, My pure devotee, under My protection, reaches the everlasting and imperishable home by My grace.

In all activities just depend upon Me and work always under My protection. In such devotional service, be fully conscious of Me.

If you become conscious of Me, you will pass over all the obstacles of conditional life by My grace. If, however, you do not work in such consciousness but act through false ego, not hearing Me, you will be lost.

If you do not act according to My direction and do not fight, then you will be falsely directed. By your nature, you will have to be engaged in warfare.

Under false belief you are now declining to act according to My direction. But, forced by the work born of your own nature, you will act all the same, O son of Kunti.

The Supreme Lord is situated in everyone's heart, O Arjuna, and is directing the wanderings of all living entities, who are seated as on a machine, made of the material energy.

O descendant of Bharata, surrender unto Him utterly. By His grace you will attain transcendental peace and the supreme and eternal home.

Thus I have explained to you knowledge still more confidential. Consider on this fully, and then do what you wish to do.

Because you are My very dear friend, I am speaking to you My supreme instruction, the most confidential knowledge of all. Hear this from Me, for it is for your benefit.

Always think of Me, become My devotee, worship Me and offer your respect unto Me. Thus you will come to Me without fail. I promise you this because you are My very dear friend.

Abandon all varieties of religion and just surrender unto Me. I shall deliver you from all sinful reactions. Do not fear.

This confidential knowledge may never be explained to those who are not serious, or devoted, or engaged in devotional service, nor to one who is jealous of Me.

For one who explains this supreme secret to the devotees, pure devotional service is guaranteed, and at the end he will come back to Me.

There is no servant in this world more dear to Me than he, nor will there ever be one more dear.

And I declare that he who studies this sacred conversation of ours worships Me by his intelligence.

And one who listens with faith and without envy becomes free from sinful reactions and attains to the auspicious planets where the pure devotee live.

O son of Pritha, O conqueror of wealth, have you heard this with an attentive mind? And are your ignorance and false believes now disappeared?

Arjuna said: My dear Krishna, O flawless one, my false belief is now gone. I have regained my memory by Your mercy. I am now firm and free from doubt and am prepared to act according to Your instructions.

Sanjaya said: Thus have I heard the conversation of two great souls, Krishna and Arjuna. And so wonderful is that message that my hair is standing on end.

By the mercy of Vyasa, I have heard these most confidential talks directly from the master of all mysticism, Krishna, who was speaking personally to Arjuna.

O King, as I repeatedly recall this wondrous and holy dialogue between Krishna and Arjuna, I take pleasure, being thrilled at every moment.

O King, as I remember the wonderful form of Lord Krishna, I am struck with wonder more and more, and I rejoice again and again.

Wherever there is Krishna, the master of all mystics, and wherever there is Arjuna, the supreme archer, there will also certainly be great wealth, victory, extraordinary power, and principles concerning the distinction between right and wrong. That is my opinion.

Let Me Now Summarize Chapter 18:

Lord Krishna explains the meaning of renunciation and what exactly is renounced order of life. Lord Krishna further explains according to the modes of nature what is knowledge, action, performer of action, understanding, determination and happiness. Lord also mentioned that a person can become perfect by following the qualities born of his own nature. The actual truth is the Supreme Personality of Godhead, Krishna. The Absolute Truth is realized in three ways—impersonal Brahman, localized Paramatma, and ultimately the Supreme Personality of Godhead, Krishna.

Lord Krishna explains Brahman realization and the ultimate conclusion of the Gita: One can understand Him as the Supreme Personality of Godhead only by pure devotional service and enables one to return to Krishna's eternal spiritual abode. In all activities, just work for Krishna, depend on Krishna, and become fully conscious of Krishna, this way you will pass through all obstacles of conditioned life else you will be lost. Lord Krishna is seated in everyone's heart and is directing all the wandering living entities. So surrender unto Lord Krishna, who will free us from all sins and by His grace you will achieve transcendental peace, come to Him and return back to His eternal abode.

I asked everyone, "Can anyone tell me what do you understand from this chapter?" One participant replied, "We understood what renunciation is, the Absolute Truth, one can understand Lord only by pure devotional service and our ultimate objective is to return to Lord Krishna's spiritual home." Another participant asked, "Madam every chapter it taught us something related to our life. Can you tell us what is this chapter all about as I have also heard that 18th Chapter is the most important chapter of The Bhagavad Gita." I said, "Indeed it is. Let me tell you something very interesting.

Journey From Head To Heart

"You are not good enough, you just cannot do it, forget it", said the head. "Hey you are a wonderful person, go ahead achieve your dreams, do not fear, do not worry, just do it", said the heart. Now you are confused whom to listen to 'the head or the heart'. "The Supreme Lord is situated in everyone's heart and is directing all the wandering human beings", said Lord Krishna to Arjuna in the Bhagavad Gita. Life is a beautiful journey from head to heart.

Few years back, as I was discovering my own thoughts I happen to realize that there are two voices that speaks with us. One comes from the analytical logical side that is our brain or head, the other voice comes from the feeling or emotional side that is our heart. I was still confused and couldn't understand which voice to listen to, which is right and will help me take the right decision. Then one day, a thought came to me of writing down all the questions to which I wanted answers. I sat down to write with a calm and peaceful mind with silence all around. To my surprise as soon as I wrote the questions, the answers started coming and I started writing them down. These answers came directly from my heart and were the right one. So never remain confused in life, clear your self doubts in your head by listening to your heart.

Many years back, there was a young son who was given the responsibility of running his father's business, which sold products that were unique. His father had set up another business for the elder son, which sold products that were common. Slowly as years passed by the elder son's business increased ten folds because of the products he was selling and the young son's business progressed slowly. Many relatives came and told the young son about how slow his business is doing as compared to the elder son's business and provoked him to change the products he was selling or shift his business elsewhere. But the young son kept on working and he never let any self doubt enter his mind or any comparison anxiety trouble him. He always remained satisfied with whatever business he did. Slowly his business excelled and he became known for the unique products he sold. One day the young son's distant cousin came to meet him at his work and she praised him for continuing his work for so many years, unlike her husband who couldn't stick to any one work and left the family struggling for money for many years. So never give an entry to the outside world to place the bomb of self-doubt into your head, just keep doing your work religiously by listening to your heart.

Around 10 years back, a father was keen to get her daughter married and settle down. Under pressure the girl advertised in local newspaper and matrimonial sites. They shortlisted one from many profiles. The boy and his family portrayed to come from a very rich, affluent family and they brain washed the girl and her father with false promises and documents. Slowly the boy made up a false story and started extracting money from the girl in pretext of urgent money required for his father's cancer treatment. One emotional blackmail lead to another until that group of son, father and many others were successful in conning the family by extracting 3 lakhs on pretext of marriage never to return. In such a situation the girl was constantly struggling to understand who is right the head or heart or both. Her head told her the boy and his family picture looks too rosy to be true and her heart told her something is not right, but still the girl and her father did what was against their inner voice and landed up in deep trouble. So when something is not right, both head and heart are always right.

Many a times, we tend to loose our self-confidence when we give the power of our happiness to someone else. There was a girl who was good looking and beautiful. But she felt sad and unhappy from inside. She had a boyfriend who never complimented her. Slowly she started loosing her self-confidence. All her other friends praised her every time but she just wanted to hear those praises and appreciation from the one whom she loved the most. Then one day, she decided to appreciate and compliment herself instead of waiting for someone else to praise her. She started talking to her own self by complimenting when she looked really good and when she did something well. She also made improvements in areas that needed attention. Slowly her self confidence boosted and now compliments doesn't matter to her because she has become flawless beauty from within. Choose to love and appreciate yourself for what you are and you will easily travel the journey from head to heart.

One day, a husband and wife were returning from a party at night. The husband had drinks, good food and had a good time. He was in an amazing and happy mood. So his wife took the opportunity to ask him his secret of being happy. She asked, "Darling I am delighted to see you at your best today, what's your secret? Are you having an affair with someone?" Husband smiled and replied, "Sweetheart I am in love with my own self. I do things that I enjoy and love the most. I only choose to be with good and positive people. I love myself first than you and our children." His wife was amazed and happy to know this, which made her fall in love with her husband all over again. So when there is self-love there is no room for self-doubt, journey of life is from the head station to the destination of your heart.

In today's time its very important for us to clear our head from all the self doubts that arise time and again. Never remain confused in life, keep working religiously, when something is not right listen to your head and heart, love and appreciate yourselves first. In the Bhagavad Gita, on the battlefield of Kurukshetra Arjuna who was a perfect warrior also faced self-doubt. His emotion towards his blood relatives was stopping him from fighting the war, which he was destined to win. Giving up his very duty of fighting was the best thing he could think of doing. Lord Krishna then came in to help Arjuna come out of this dilemma. He narrated him 'The Bhagavad Gita', wherein Lord Krishna takes him on a journey from head to the heart. Here comes another life lesson.

**Lesson No: 38 Never be confused in life. Never give up doing your duties, keep working religiously without any expectations of success or failure. Love and appreciate yourself first. Listen to your heart.

One participant raised his hand and asked, "Madam can you summarize the entire Bhagavad Gita in short?" Another participant said, "We all have liked the stories of Lord Krishna and want to hear more." I smiled and said, "Here comes an interesting story which I want to share it with all of you.

The Boatmen

One day Lord Krishna was in a forest, he saw a big river and wanted to cross that river and go on the other side. All of a sudden a boatman came to help Lord Krishna cross the river.

"What is your price?" asks Lord Krishna.

"Just get onto my boat and we will deal with the payment later", said the boatman.

Lord Krishna gets on the boat and then the boatman goes across the river. All the time while he was rowing, he looks at Lord Krishna and tears of love stream from his eyes.

Lord Krishna asked the boatman, "Why are you crying?" The boatman replied, "It's my honor and privilege to be of help to you My Lord. I wish to always keep serving you and come to your abode after death. But I know it's not possible, I'm just an ordinary boatman and you are the Supreme Lord."

Lord Krishna smiled and said, "Every human being is most welcome to My abode. I eagerly wait for my devotees to come to my abode. The only thing stops them is their own belief. They must have a strong desire to come to My home."

The boatman further asked, "But how can an ordinary boatman like me come to Your home?"

Lord Krishna said, "If you are a boatman or a businessman or a butcher or an artist or a service person, one must continue doing his job and duties as a household. He must do so without any expectation or attachment for its benefits or results. One must never give up or renounce his duties. When you do not give up the fruits or benefits as a result of your work, you carry it after death. But one who has given up the fruits or benefits and attachments has nothing to suffer or enjoy after death."

"Do your duty without any ego, with great determination and enthusiasm, without wavering in success or failure. One must have the understanding of what needs to be done, what not needs to be done, what is to be feared and what is not to be feared. Your determination should be unbreakable. You should also be able to control your body, mind and speech. Be detached from anger, sexual desire, greed, false pride and attachment."

"When you see Me present in each and every living being that's knowledge. True happiness comes from self-realization and not by satisfying your senses. You can understand Me only by pure devotional service. When you are fully conscious of Me, then you can enter My kingdom My abode. I am situated in everyone's heart and directing all the wandering living beings. Always think of Me, surrender unto Me, worship Me, offer your respect unto Me and by My grace you will experience peace and come to My home."

The boatman thanks Lord Krishna for his guidance. Then the boatman rows and rows.

Finally, they arrive on the other side of the river. Lord Krishna looks at the beautiful pearls around his neck. He then gives this very valuable pearl necklace to the boatman and says:

This is My payment.

But the boatman responds as follows:

"No, no, no, no, no! Please keep it! Keep it! Did you not know that in this part of your country, the boatmen have an agreement amongst themselves: one boatman will never accept payment from another boatman."

"Since when have I become a boatman?" asks Lord Krishna.

"Oh, You are a boatman! See, I am a tiny ordinary boatman. I take passengers on my old boat from one side of the river to the other. But you are a big boatman! You take the souls to their real home on your personal boat and help them cross the ocean of birth and death. But please remember that when I come to your ocean, please don't ask for any payment from me, just remember that we are boatmen and we had a deal!"

Lord Krishna smiled and said, "Let it be so. When you come to the shores of the ocean of birth and death, I will take you onto my boat and no payment will be required."

Finally in the Bhagavad Gita, Lord Krishna tells Arjuna that the person who studies our scared conversation, worships Me by his intelligence. Also, the one who listens to this conversation with faith and without discontent becomes free from all sinful reactions. Lord Krishna reconfirms with Arjuna that has he listened with an attentive mind and has his lack of knowledge and false belief disappeared. Arjuna confirms to Lord Krishna that his false belief is gone. He is now firm and free from doubt and prepared to act according to Lord Krishna's instructions. Here come the last life lessons.

Lesson No: 39 One must have a strong desire to reach God. Lord Krishna Himself takes care of his devotees by helping them cross the

ocean of birth and death. Read or listen the sacred Bhagavad Gita with faith and you will become free from all sinful reactions.

**Lesson No: 40 Stay Happy, Stay Blessed. Share this knowledge with everyone.

Hope you all have enjoyed the 2-day spiritual session on The Bhagavad Gita. Everyone happily nodded. One participant said, "We want to listen to more stories and life lessons, we are still feeling empty and want to gain more knowledge." Everyone started shouting, "More, we want more." Another participant said, "Madam there was no exercise or game or surprise element in this chapter?" I said, "This session is still not over my dear participants."

I said, "It time for writing your feedback. I would request everyone to please write and let me know how this session was and any improvements or suggestions from your side you can mention in the comments."

After the feedback forms were submitted. "It's now time to head to the beach just outside our resort, I have a surprise planned for all of you."

Everyone assembled on the beach in no time. It was late evening and the sun was setting down. I handed over paper lanterns to all participants. "Now you all need to light your own paper lantern and release it up in the air. Let go all your worries, let go all that has been stopping you as you release your respective lanterns up into the sky. Hey come together, time to take a group selfie."

Author

Sheetal Khurana, an avid motivational speaker, author, life coach and career growth consultant inspires people to live a happy confident life. Her learning comes from divine teachings of The Bhagavad Gita that she believes can help in our modern times.

She is an enthusiastic toastmaster at Toastmasters for Pune Entrepreneurs and has won numerous accolades as best speaker. She conducts various signature programs for personal mastery, career development and spiritual development for personal and professional growth. Individuals and corporates have benefitted through her Gita Happiness programs and retreats, at various destinations. Sheetal is passionate about sharing her knowledge on The Bhagavad Gita, besides enjoys travelling and watching movies.

An entrepreneur with 14 years of experience as recruitment consultant, she trains fresher and experienced job seekers on job search strategies and techniques to help them find right placements.

Know more visit her at www.sheetalkhurana.com

CPSIA information can be obtained
at www.ICGtesting.com
Printed in the USA
BVHW031818020820
585289BV00001B/8